Heart & Home Expressions™

Edited by Laura Scott

HOUSE of
WHITE
BIRCHES
PUBLISHERS
SINCE 1947

Editor: Laura Scott
Associate Editor: June Sprunger
Copy Editor: Cathy Reef
Photography: Nora Elsesser, Tammy Christian
Photography Assistant: Linda Quinlan

Production Manager: Vicki Macy
Creative Coordinator: Shaun Venish
Book Design: Becky Sarasin
Book Production: Dan Kraner
Production Coordinator: Sandra Beres
Production Assistants: Cheryl Lynch, Darren Powell, Jessica Rothe, Miriam Zacharias

Publishers: Carl H. Muselman, Arthur K. Muselman
Chief Executive Officer: John Robinson
Marketing Director: Scott Moss
Editorial Director: Vivian Rothe
Production Director: Scott Smith

Printed in the United States of America
First Printing: 1997
Library of Congress Number: 96-78455
ISBN: 1-882138-22-8

Every effort has been made to ensure the accuracy and completeness of the
instructions in this book. However, we cannot be responsible for human
error or for the results when using materials other than those specified in
the instructions, or for variations in individual work.

Cover project: Classic Vanity Set, page 130

A WARM WELCOME

Since plastic canvas became a popular needlecraft in the early 1980s, we've seen it bloom into a craft every bit as lovely as traditional needlecrafts such as cross-stitch, quilting and needlepoint.

In your hands you hold a showcase of plastic canvas designs that will please you as a needlecrafter and also fulfill your home decorating creativity. This volume brings you literally dozens (more than 70!) of brand-new, never-before-published designs perfect for giving your home a decorator's touch.

Our designers rose above the challenge to bring plastic canvas to yet a higher level of quality and beauty. Warm kitchen accents and table settings, cozy family room games and samplers, whimsical children's projects, handy bathroom and vanity accessories, home office helpers and beautiful designs for the bedroom are all designed with a grace and style sure to please you and your loved ones.

Express your creativity and style with plastic canvas— and let it warm your heart and your home.

Warm regards,

Laura Scott

Editor

CONTENTS

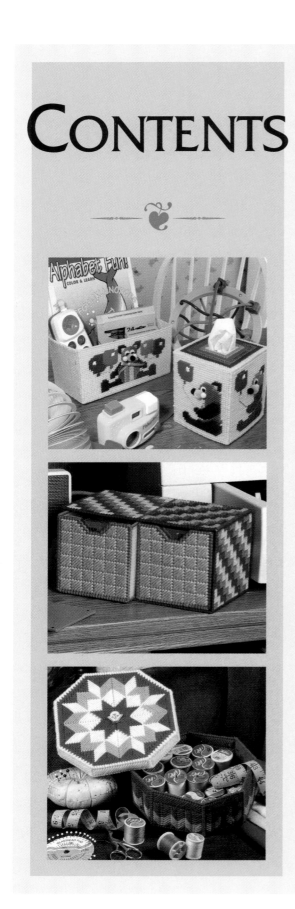

CONTENTS

Chapter One

KITCHEN STITCHERY

*This first chapter of
Heart & Home Expressions
will turn your kitchen into the
family's favorite gathering
spot for sharing the day's
adventures. Filled not only
with warm, inviting aromas,
but also with the many
cheerful decorations included
in this chapter, your kitchen
will beautifully express the
love you feel for your family.*

Floral Mugs

*A beautiful spring bouquet and a trio of irises
adorn these easy-to-stitch mug inserts. They make
lovely gifts for coffee or tea drinkers!*

Skill Level: Advanced beginner

Spring Bouquet

Materials
- ⅓ sheet 10-count plastic canvas
- 6-strand embroidery floss as listed in color key
- Tapestry needle
- White-rimmed plastic mug with insert area

Instructions
1. Cut plastic canvas according to graph (page 9).

2. Continental Stitch piece with 12 strands floss following graph, stitching flower designs first and cream background next. Backstitch with 3 strands medium mustard over completed Continental Stitches.

3. Whipstitch short edges together with 12 strands cream floss. Overcast remaining edges with 6 strands of cream floss.

4. Insert stitched piece in mug with seam at handle.

Trio of Irises

Materials
- ⅓ sheet 10-count plastic canvas
- 6-strand embroidery floss as listed in color key
- Tapestry needle
- White-rimmed plastic mug with insert area

Instructions
1. Cut plastic canvas according to graph below.

2. Continental Stitch piece with 12 strands floss following graph, stitching design area first and navy background last.

3. Whipstitch short edges together with 12 strands navy. Overcast remaining edges with 6 strands navy.

4. Insert stitched piece in mug with seam at handle.

—Designed by Kathleen Marie O'Donnell

Trio of Irises
94 holes x 35 holes
Cut 1

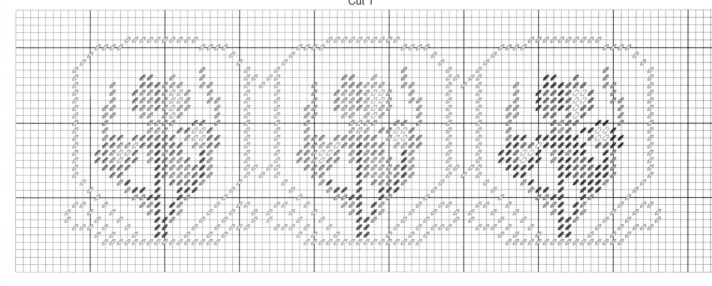

Spring Bouquet
94 holes x 36 holes
Cut 1

FLORAL MUGS

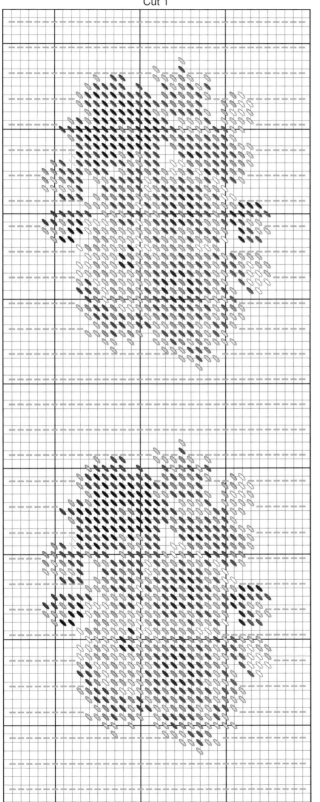

COOKING ANGEL

*You'll always have help in the kitchen
with this sweet angel on hand!*

Skill Level: Advanced beginner

Materials
- 2 sheets 7-count plastic canvas
- Worsted weight yarn as listed in color key
- #16 tapestry needle
- Ceramic tulip heart button #86062
- 4" ⅛"-wide light blue double-faced satin ribbon
- #24 tapestry needle and white embroidery floss or thread
- 5½" white doll stand #7380A
- Hot-glue gun

Instructions

1. Cut plastic canvas according to graph. Back piece will remain unstitched.

2. Stitch angel front following graph. Work embroidery with 2 plies yarn over completed background stitching.

3. Using photo as a guide throughout, center and sew button to top part of apron with #24 tapestry needle and white floss or thread. Tie blue satin ribbon in a bow and glue to collar. Trim ends as desired.

4. With white, Overcast bottom edge of front piece. Whipstitch angel front and back together at ruffle side edges and wings with white, hat with pearl gray, hair with tapestry gold, navy border on skirt with navy, and remaining skirt and arm edges with deep Colonial blue.

5. Remove ring insert from top of doll stand and discard. Insert doll stand in opening at bottom of angel.

—Designed by Joan Green

COLOR KEY	
Worsted Weight Yarn	**Yards**
▨ Honey #8795	2
■ Deep Colonial blue #8860	10
▨ Pale Colonial blue #8863	16
▨ Light tapestry gold #8886	2
■ Pearl gray #8912	3
▨ Rose #8921	2
☐ White #8942	18
■ Navy #8965	5
▨ Light peach #8977	2
Uncoded areas are white #8942 Continental Stitches	
╱ Walnut #8916 Backstitch	1
● Walnut #8916 French Knot	
● Rose #8921 French Knot	
╱ Navy #8965 Straight Stitch	
Color numbers given are for Spinrite Bernat Berella "4" worsted weight yarn.	

Cooking Angel
50 holes x 78 hole
Cut 2, stitch 1

COUNTRY KITCHEN

*Let your family and friends know that yours is a
genuine country cooking kitchen with this eye-catching sign!*

Skill Level: Beginner

Materials

- ½ artist-size sheet 7-count plastic canvas
- Worsted weight yarn as listed in color key
- #16 tapestry needle
- 14½" x 5½" piece cardboard
- Sawtooth hanger
- Hot-glue gun

Instructions

1. Cut plastic canvas according to graph below.

2. Stitch plastic canvas following graph. For far right utensil, work handle in Cross Stitch and top part in Continental Stitches, working Long Stitches over completed Continental Stitches. Overcast edges with deep Colonial blue.

3. Glue cardboard to backside of stitched piece. Glue sawtooth hanger to center top back of cardboard.

—*Designed by Joan Green*

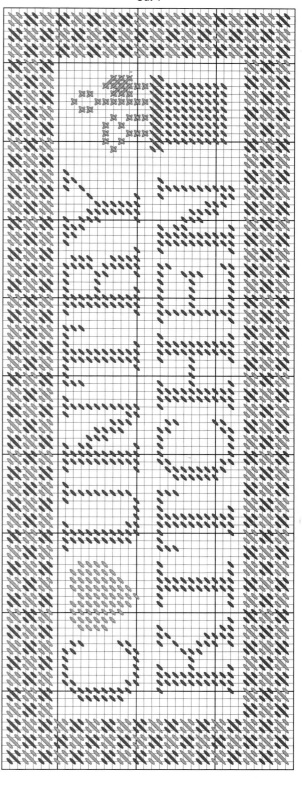

Country Kitchen
97 holes x 37 holes
Cut 1

COLOR KEY	
Worsted Weight Yarn	**Yards**
Honey #8795	2
Arbutus #8922	1
Deep Colonial blue #8860	24
Light tapestry gold #8886	12
Dark oxford gray #8893	2
Uncoded area is natural #8940 Continental Stitch	22
Color numbers given are for Spinrite Bernat Berella "4" worsted weight yarn.	

Heart & Home Expressions **13**

Herb Planter

*A bright, sunny kitchen window is the perfect place to
grow your favorite herbs nestled in this attractive planter.*

Skill Level: Advanced beginner

Materials
- 2 sheets 7-count stiff plastic canvas
- Plastic canvas yarn as listed in color key
- #3 pearl cotton as listed in color key
- Plastic
- Hot-glue gun

Project Note
Planter is large enough to hold up to three 3½"-
wide by 3½"-tall plant pots.

Instructions
1. Cut plastic canvas according to graphs (pages 15
and 16). Cut one 74-hole x 26-hole piece for planter
bottom.

2. Stitch pieces following graphs. Continental
Stitch bottom piece with curry. Backstitch letters
on signs with dark copper pearl cotton over completed Cross Stitches. *Note: Walnut Backstitches
and Straight Stitches will be added in step 4.*

3. Overcast fences with white. With walnut,
Overcast signs and top edges of front, back and sides.
With curry, Whipstitch front, back and sides togeth-
er, then Whipstitch bottom to front, back and sides.

4. Following graphs, add walnut Backstitches and
Straight Stitches to front, back and sides, wrapping
stitches around corners.

5. Using photo as a guide, glue fences to all four
sides, making sure bottom edges of fences and
planter are even; glue signs to planter front.

6. Line planter with plastic to protect yarn from
moisture of plant pots.

—Designed by Celia Lange Designs

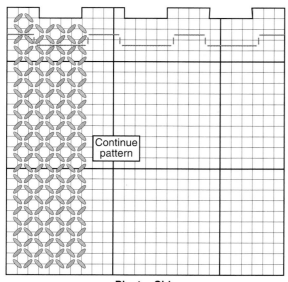

Planter Side
26 holes x 25 holes
Cut 2

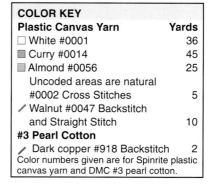

COLOR KEY	
Plastic Canvas Yarn	**Yards**
☐ White #0001	36
▨ Curry #0014	45
▨ Almond #0056	25
Uncoded areas are natural	
#0002 Cross Stitches	5
╱ Walnut #0047 Backstitch	
and Straight Stitch	10
#3 Pearl Cotton	
╱ Dark copper #918 Backstitch	2
Color numbers given are for Spinrite plastic canvas yarn and DMC #3 pearl cotton.	

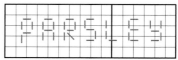

Parsley Sign
16 holes x 5 holes
Cut 1

HERB PLANTER

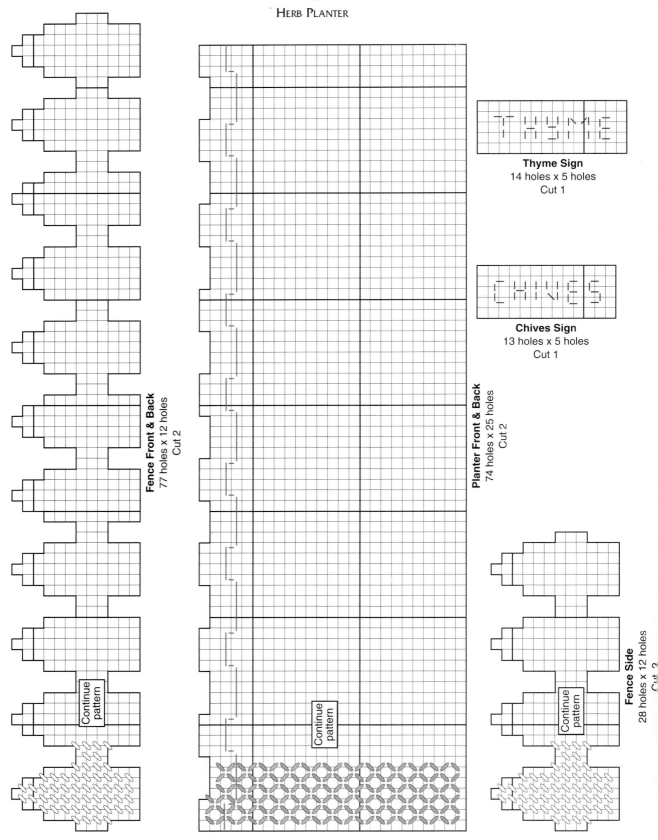

Fence Front & Back
77 holes x 12 holes
Cut 2

Continue pattern

Planter Front & Back
74 holes x 25 holes
Cut 2

Continue pattern

Thyme Sign
14 holes x 5 holes
Cut 1

Chives Sign
13 holes x 5 holes
Cut 1

Fence Side
28 holes x 12 holes
Cut 2

Continue pattern

SUGAR 'N' SPICE

A collection of all the baking essentials and a cheerful flowered ribbon adorn a simple heart-shaped grapevine wreath for a pretty kitchen decoration.

Skill Level: Beginner

Materials

- 1 sheet 7-count stiff plastic canvas
- Plastic canvas yarn as listed in color key
- #3 pearl cotton as listed in color key
- 14" heart-shaped grapevine wreath
- 4 yards 1½"-wide coordinating ribbon (sample used flowered ribbon)
- Plastic-coated wire
- Hot-glue gun

Instructions

1. Cut plastic canvas according to graphs (pages 17 and 18).

2. Continental Stitch pieces following graphs. Do not work embroidery at this time. Overcast milk pitcher and sugar bowl with white, herb bottle with silver gray, spice jar lid with mustard, and recipe card and spice jar with rust.

3. Work embroidery over completed Continental Stitching and Overcasting where indicated. Wrap a 6½" length of rust yarn around neck of herb bottle and tie in a bow; trim ends as desired.

4. Beginning and ending at top center, wrap ribbon around wreath and secure with hot glue and plastic-coated wire.

5. Form a multi-looped bow with remaining ribbon and attach at top center (see photo).

6. Using photo as guide, glue stitched pieces to wreath.

—Designed by Celia Lange Designs

COLOR KEY

Plastic Canvas Yarn	Yards
☐ White #0001	15
■ Black #0028	1
☐ Mustard #0043	8
▨ Silver gray #0045	3
■ Poplar #0051	4
Uncoded areas are rust #0034 Continental Stitches	8
○ White #0001 French Knot	
╱ White #0001 Backstitch	
╱ Black #0028 Backstitch	
╱ Rust #0034 Backstitch	
╱ Mustard #0043 Backstitch	
╱ Poplar #0051 Backstitch	
#3 Pearl Cotton	
╱ Black #310	4
✿ Light orange #743 Lazy Daisy	1

Color numbers given are for Spinrite plastic canvas yarn and DMC #3 pearl cotton.

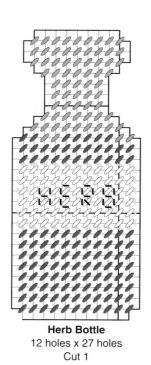

Herb Bottle
12 holes x 27 holes
Cut 1

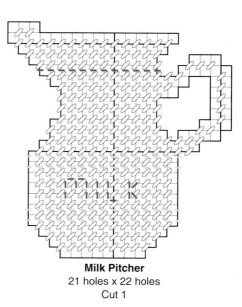

Milk Pitcher
21 holes x 22 holes
Cut 1

See photo on page 14
Graphs continued on page 19

CHICKEN LITTLE

This whimsical chicken basket is the perfect size for holding napkins, utensils and other kitchen odds and ends!

with white. Whipstitch front of chicken and top part of comb together between blue dots with adjacent colors. Overcast remaining edges of comb with red.

4. Using white through step 5, Whipstitch bottom to bottom edges of basket sides.

5. Whipstitch short edges of lining together, then insert inside basket with seam to the front. Whipstitch top edges of basket and lining together where they touch. Overcast remaining top edges of basket.

—Designed by Carole Rodgers

COLOR KEY	
Plastic Canvas Yarn	**Yards**
■ Black #00	½
■ Red #01	1
▨ Tangerine #11	4
■ Gray #38	32
☐ White #41	
Color numbers given are for Uniek Needloft plastic canvas yarn.	

Skill Level: Beginner

Materials

- 2 sheets 7-count stiff plastic canvas
- Plastic canvas yarn as listed in color key

Instructions

1. Cut plastic canvas according to graphs (pages 18 and 19). Cut one 87-hole x 24-hole piece for basket lining.

2. Stitch sides following graph, reversing one before stitching. Basket lining and bottom will remain unstitched.

3. With wrong sides of basket sides together, Whipstitch chicken tail together between blue dots

Chicken Basket Bottom
34 holes x 25 holes
Cut 2

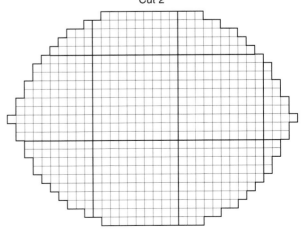

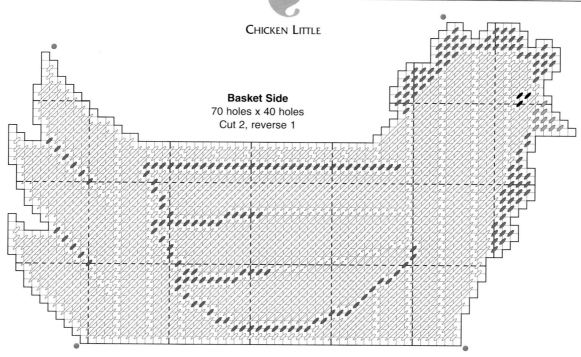

Basket Side
70 holes x 40 holes
Cut 2, reverse 1

Sugar 'n' Spice Graphs
Continued from page 17

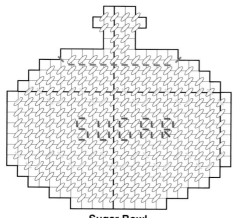

Sugar Bowl
21 holes x 19 holes
Cut 1

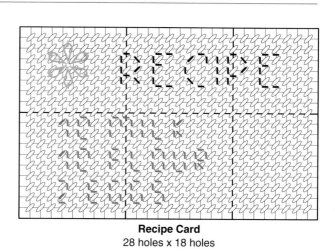

Recipe Card
28 holes x 18 holes
Cut 1

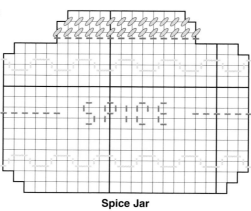

Spice Jar
23 holes x 17 holes
Cut 1

MESSAGE CENTER

Get your family's attention by adding a decorative border to your message board. Work it in the cheerful colors given or to match your kitchen.

Skill Level: Beginner

Materials
- 12" x 18" sheet 7-count stiff plastic canvas
- Plastic canvas yarn as listed in color key
- #18 tapestry needle
- #22 tapestry needle
- 4 (¾") white 4-hole buttons
- 18" 20-gauge white cloth stem wire
- 8½" x 11" dry-erase board with marker pen
- Magnetic or adhesive strips

Project Note
If desired, a chalkboard or corkboard may be substituted for the dry-erase board.

Instructions

1. Cut plastic canvas according to graph (page 22). Cut two 3-hole x 59-hole strips and two 3-hole by 75-hole strips for frame back. *Note: Depth of frame strips may be adjusted to accommodate purchased board.*

2. With #18 tapestry needle, stitch piece following graph. With white, Whipstitch short edges of frame strips together, then attach corners to border where indicated on graph.

3. With yellow, Whipstitch frame strips to border where indicated on graph, making sure to Whipstitch in same direction as previous stitching. Overcast inside edges with royal.

4. For pen holder, wrap cloth stem wire loosely around marker pen seven times, leaving approximately 2¼" straight on each end.

5. Center pen holder on bottom edge of border; Overcast bottom edge with yellow, catching straight ends of wire. Continue Overcasting outer edges with yellow.

6. Separate royal yarn into two strands. Thread #22 tapestry needle with one strand, then Cross Stitch buttons to yellow flower centers.

7. Knot one end of a 9" length of white yarn. Thread yarn through the 13th outermost hole from one corner on frame strip. Pull yarn through and wrap around bar once. Thread yarn through corresponding hole across corner, wrap yarn around bar once and knot. Repeat with remaining three corners.

8. Slip corners of dry-erase board under yarn corners. Attach magnetic or adhesive strips as desired to backside of board.

—Designed by Kathy Wirth

SPACE SAVERS

If you don't have much table or counter space, try hanging up a clear shower organizer on the wall. (They can be purchased for about $1). Organize like materials together, such as canvas shapes in one pocket, scissors in another, pom pons in another, etc. With see-through pockets, you'll never have to dig through drawers or boxes of craft supplies again!

Save empty 16 oz cracker boxes and use them to store your 8 oz skeins of yarn. By dropping the yarn in the box with the starting thread on top, you can see the color and work with the yarn without ever removing it from the box!

CRAFTING FOR $$$

When making magnets, make one out of 7-count canvas and another out of 10-count canvas. The smaller piece makes a great magnet, too, or can be used as a pin.

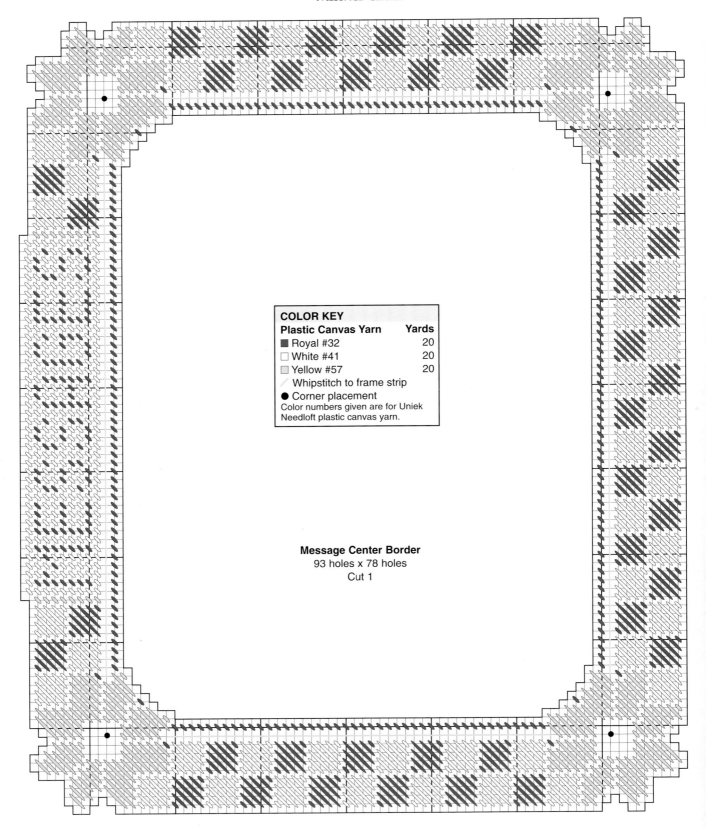

COLOR KEY

Plastic Canvas Yarn	Yards
■ Royal #32	20
□ White #41	20
□ Yellow #57	20
╱ Whipstitch to frame strip	
● Corner placement	

Color numbers given are for Uniek Needloft plastic canvas yarn.

Message Center Border
93 holes x 78 holes
Cut 1

GARDEN-FRESH CADDIES

Four whimsical wall caddies, including a carrot, a pea pod, an ear of corn and a bean, will dress up your walls and help you to stay organized!

Skill Level: Intermediate

Materials

All Projects
- Plastic canvas yarn as listed in color key
- #18 tapestry needle
- Sewing needle and thread
- Sawtooth hanger or magnets
- Hot-glue gun

Carrot Coupon Holder
- 1 sheet 7-count plastic canvas
- 5½" 1½"-wide white lace
- 1¼"-wide lace-trimmed hair bow

Peas Key-per
- 1 sheet 7-count plastic canvas
- 6" ⅛"-wide ivory satin ribbon
- 3 green paper clips

Bean Bag Lady
- 1 sheet 7-count plastic canvas
- 13" ½"-wide white lace
- 1½"-wide lace-trimmed hair bow
- Plastic sandwich bags

Corny Communications Center
- 2 sheets 7-count plastic canvas
- 1¾" navy bow tie
- 18mm ruby global faceted bead
- 10mm emerald faceted bead
- Small notepad
- Pen and pencil

CARROT COUPON HOLDER

1. Cut plastic canvas according to graphs (pages 25 and 26).

2. Stitch pieces following graphs. Part of the carrot will remain unstitched. Work embroidery over completed background stitching.

3. Overcast leaf with apple green and top edge of pocket with light orange. Place pocket on unstitched area of carrot, aligning edges. Whipstitch bottom edge of pocket to carrot with light orange.

4. With orange, Whipstitch side edges of pocket and carrot together, Overcasting remaining edges of carrot.

5. Using photo as a guide and sewing needle and thread throughout, attach small hair bow to base of leaf. Sew lace collar to carrot below face and above pocket, wrapping lace around sides and attaching to backside.

6. Sew sawtooth hanger or glue magnets to backside of carrot.

PEAS KEY-PER

1. Cut plastic canvas according to graphs (page 26).

2. Stitch pieces following graphs. Work embroidery over completed background stitching.

3. Overcast all pieces with brisk green, attaching paper clips to peas while Overcasting (see photo). Using photo as a guide, center and attach peas to pod with brisk green at equal intervals below mouth.

4. Tie ivory ribbon in a bow. With sewing needle and thread, attach bow to pea pod just above top pea. Trim ends as desired.

5. Sew sawtooth hanger or glue magnets to backside of pea pod.

6. Hang keys from clips.

BEAN BAG LADY

1. Cut plastic canvas according to graphs (page 27).

2. Stitch pieces following graphs. Part of the bean will remain unstitched. Work embroidery over completed background stitching.

3. With brisk green, Overcast inside edge and adjacent top edge to red dot on each pocket.

4. Cut lace in half. Using photo as a guide, with sewing needle and thread, attach lace along the inside edge of each pocket, wrapping lace over Overcast portion of top edge. Sew remaining portion of lace to backside.

5. Place pockets over unstitched portion of bean, aligning edges. Using brisk green through step 6, Whipstitch bottom edge and remaining sections of top edges of pockets to bean.

6. Whipstitch side edges of pockets and bean together, Overcasting remaining edges of bean.

7. With sewing needle and thread, sew hair bow to curl on forehead.

8. Sew sawtooth hanger or glue magnets to backside of bean.

9. Tuck sandwich bags into pockets.

Corny Communications Center

1. Cut plastic canvas according to graphs (page 28).

2. Stitch pieces following graphs. Part of the main body will remain unstitched. Work embroidery over completed background stitching.

3. Using brisk green through step 4, Overcast inside and top edges of husk. Do not Overcast edges between dots. Overcast top edges of main body.

4. Place husk over main body, aligning edges. Whipstitch inside edges on each leaf of husk between dots to main body. Whipstitch outside edges together.

5. Using photo as a guide, with sewing needle and thread, sew bow tie under mouth. With green yarn, attach ruby, then emerald, beads to center top of head.

6. Sew sawtooth hanger or glue magnets to back-side of main body.

7. Insert pen and pencil in vertical pockets at top of husk. Tuck notepad into pocket area under bow tie.

—Designed by Carol Krob

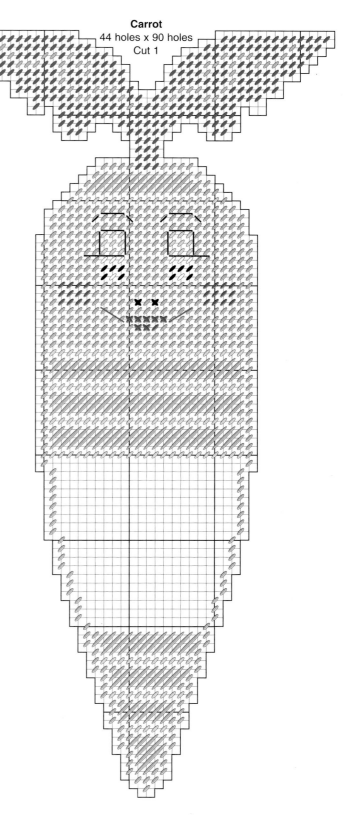

Carrot
44 holes x 90 holes
Cut 1

COLOR KEY
CARROT COUPON HOLDER

Plastic Canvas Yarn	Yards
☐ White #0001	1
■ Wine #0011	1
■ Brisk green #0027	5
■ Black #0028	1
▨ Orange #0030	18
☐ Light orange #0038	3
▨ Apple #0041	3
╱ Wine #0011 Straight Stitch	
╱ Black #0028 Straight Stitch	

Color numbers given are for Spinrite plastic canvas yarn.

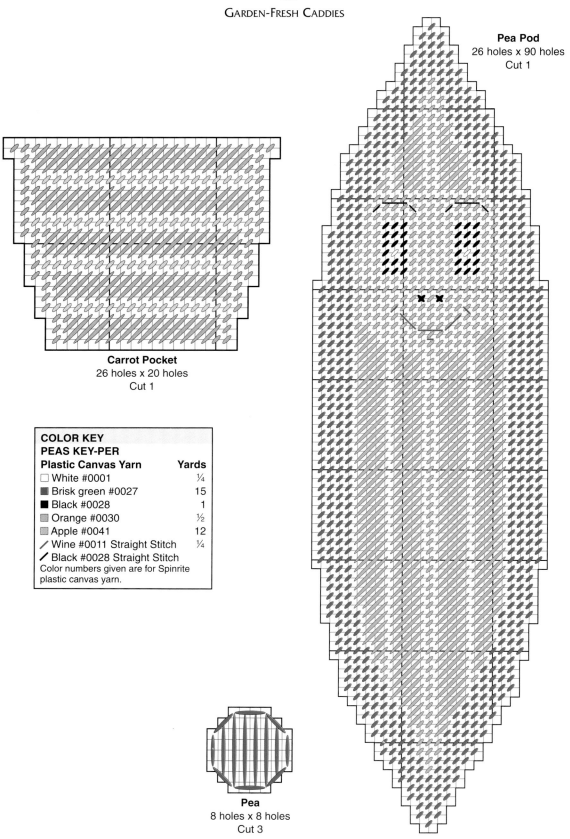

Pea Pod
26 holes x 90 holes
Cut 1

Carrot Pocket
26 holes x 20 holes
Cut 1

COLOR KEY
PEAS KEY-PER

Plastic Canvas Yarn	Yards
☐ White #0001	¼
■ Brisk green #0027	15
■ Black #0028	1
▨ Orange #0030	½
▨ Apple #0041	12
╱ Wine #0011 Straight Stitch	¼
╱ Black #0028 Straight Stitch	

Color numbers given are for Spinrite plastic canvas yarn.

Pea
8 holes x 8 holes
Cut 3

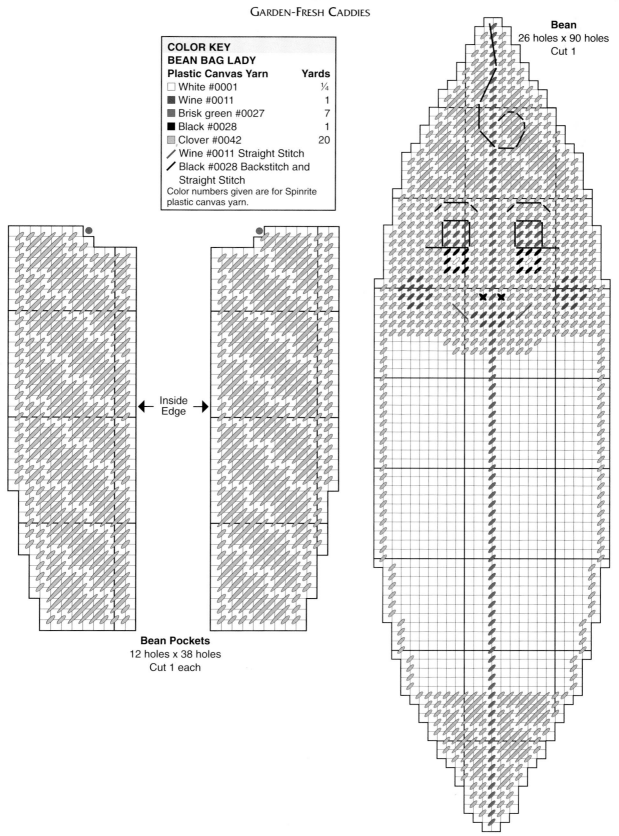

COLOR KEY
BEAN BAG LADY

Plastic Canvas Yarn	Yards
☐ White #0001	¼
■ Wine #0011	1
■ Brisk green #0027	7
■ Black #0028	1
▨ Clover #0042	20
╱ Wine #0011 Straight Stitch	
╱ Black #0028 Backstitch and Straight Stitch	

Color numbers given are for Spinrite plastic canvas yarn.

Bean
26 holes x 90 holes
Cut 1

← Inside Edge →

Bean Pockets
12 holes x 38 holes
Cut 1 each

COLOR KEY
CORNY COMMUNICATIONS CENTER

Plastic Canvas Yarn	Yards
☐ White #0001	¼
■ Wine #0011	1
■ Brisk green #0027	15
■ Black #0028	1
☐ Daffodil #0029	6
■ Orange #0030	¼
■ Apple #0041	20
■ Mustard #0043	6
╱ Wine #0011 Straight Stitch	
╱ Black #0028 Straight Stitch	

Color numbers given are for Spinrite plastic canvas yarn.

Corn Main Body
44 holes x 90 holes
Cut 1

Corn Husk
44 holes x 90 holes
Cut 1

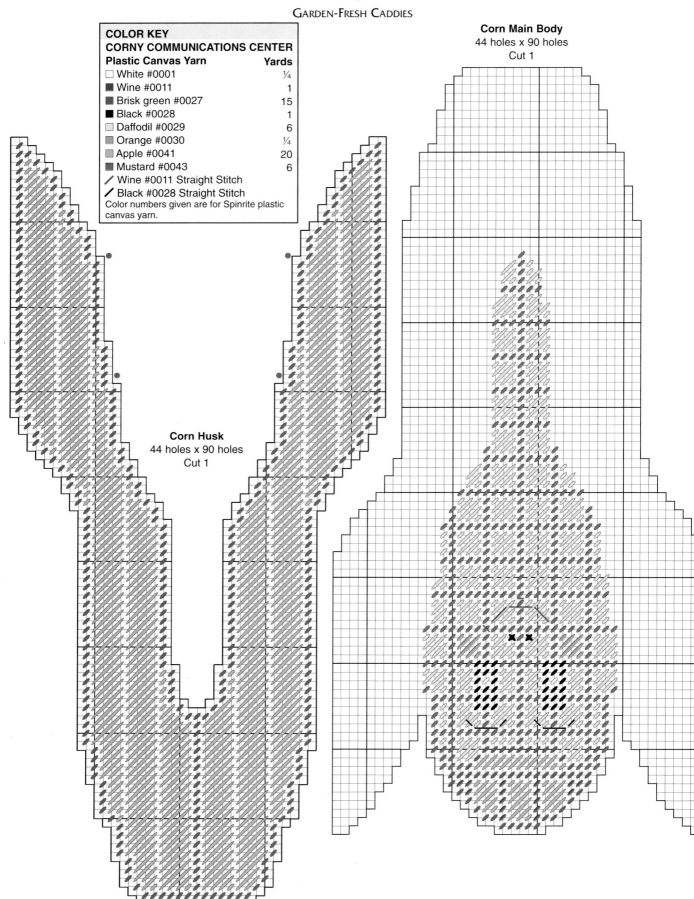

KITCHEN STITCHERY

FRUIT COASTER SET

This set of four classy coasters pictures a pear,
an apple, a bunch of grapes and a peach worked in
shades of pearl cotton on 10-count plastic canvas.

Skill Level: Advanced beginner

Materials
- ⅔ sheet 10-count plastic canvas
- 6-strand embroidery floss as listed in color key
- Tapestry needle
- 4 (4") squares ivory felt
- Sewing needle

Instructions

1. Cut plastic canvas according to graphs (pages 30–32).

2. Continental Stitch coasters with 12 strands floss following graphs. Overcast edges with 6 strands olive green floss.

3. Stitch ivory felt to back of coasters with sewing needle and 1 strand ivory floss.

—Designed by Kathleen Marie O'Donnell

Apple
41 holes x 41 holes
Cut 1

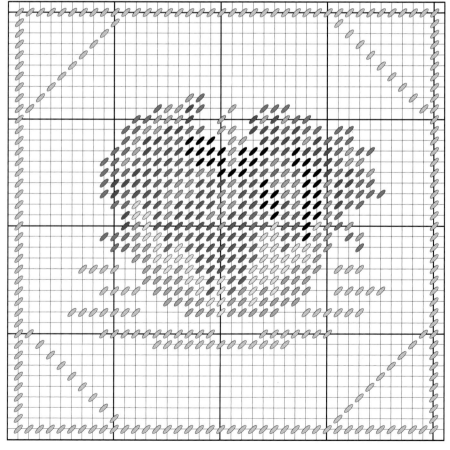

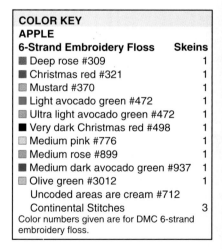

COLOR KEY	
APPLE	
6-Strand Embroidery Floss	**Skeins**
■ Deep rose #309	1
■ Christmas red #321	1
▨ Mustard #370	1
■ Light avocado green #472	1
▨ Ultra light avocado green #472	1
■ Very dark Christmas red #498	1
▢ Medium pink #776	1
▨ Medium rose #899	1
■ Medium dark avocado green #937	1
▢ Olive green #3012	1
Uncoded areas are cream #712	
Continental Stitches	3
Color numbers given are for DMC 6-strand embroidery floss.	

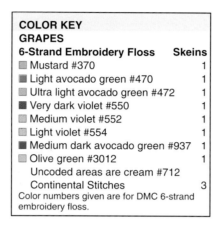

COLOR KEY
GRAPES

6-Strand Embroidery Floss	Skeins
Mustard #370	1
Light avocado green #470	1
Ultra light avocado green #472	1
Very dark violet #550	1
Medium violet #552	1
Light violet #554	1
Medium dark avocado green #937	1
Olive green #3012	1
Uncoded areas are cream #712 Continental Stitches	3

Color numbers given are for DMC 6-strand embroidery floss.

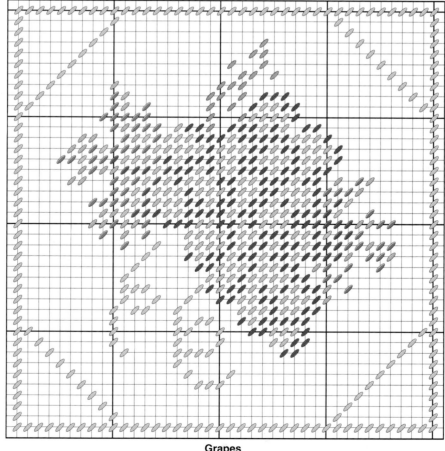

Grapes
41 holes x 41 holes
Cut 1

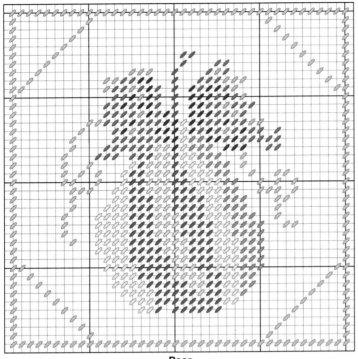

COLOR KEY
PEAR

6-Strand Embroidery Floss	Skeins
■ Mustard #370	1
■ Light avocado green #470	1
▨ Ultra light avocado green #472	1
☐ Deep canary #725	1
■ Light topaz #726	1
☐ Very light topaz #727	1
▨ Bright gold #783	1
■ Medium dark avocado green #937	1
▨ Olive green #3012	1
Uncoded areas are cream #712	
Continental Stitches	1

Color numbers given are for DMC 6-strand embroidery floss.

Pear
41 holes x 41 holes
Cut 1

COLOR KEY
PEACH

6-Strand Embroidery Floss	Skeins
▨ Mustard #370	1
■ Light avocado green #470	1
▨ Ultra light avocado green #472	1
■ Light orange spice #722	1
■ Medium dark avocado green #937	1
▨ Olive green #3012	1
▨ Medium apricot #3341	1
☐ Light apricot #3824	1
Uncoded areas are cream #712	
Continental Stitches	3

Color numbers given are for DMC 6-strand embroidery floss.

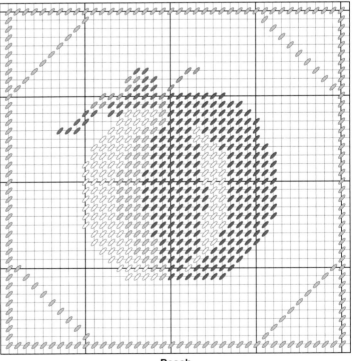

Peach
41 holes x 41 holes
Cut 1

MAPLE LEAF TABLE SET

Strips of colorful cotton fabric worked on 5-count canvas
make for an unusual, rustic table set perfect for relaxed dining!

Skill Level: Advanced beginner

Materials

- 2 artist-size sheets 5-count plastic canvas
- ¾" strips cotton or cotton/polyester 45"-wide fabric:
  20 strips off-white with small Wedgwood blue pattern
  31 strips yellow gold
  29 strips berry print
  24 strips Wedgwood blue print
  16 strips jade print
- Tapestry needle
- 4" x 10" piece coordinating felt (optional)
- Hot-glue gun (optional)

Project Notes

Choose fabric with simple, shaded patterns of the specified color or with an off-white pattern. Avoid using multicolored prints. Solid color fabrics may be substituted if desired.

Prewash fabric if desired. Prepare strips by marking every ¾" along one selvage edge. Snip each mark with scissors to start tear. Hold fabric firmly at each cut and pull to tear into strips. Discard first and last strips if they are not ¾" wide. Remove extra-long threads from strips.

Use scissors-cut end or fold fabric when threading needle. Secure strip ends under stitches on backside as though stitching with yarn. When stitching, untwist fabric as necessary to keep right side showing. *Note: Wrong side of fabric will show at times.*

Instructions

1. Cut plastic canvas according to graphs (pages 34 and 35). Centerpiece box bottom will remain unstitched.

2. Work all vertical and horizontal stitches following graphs. Add berry print Straight Stitches when background stitching is completed.

3. Overcast place mat with berry print. Whipstitch short edges of napkin ring together with Wedgwood blue; Overcast remaining edges with yellow gold.

4. Using berry print throughout, Overcast top edges of centerpiece box sides. Whipstitch box sides together, then Whipstitch sides to bottom. If desired, glue felt to box bottom.

—Designed by Nancy Marshall

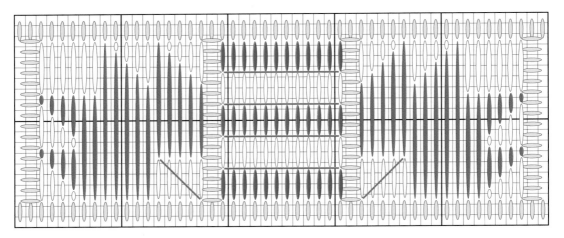

Centerpiece Box
Large Side & Bottom
50 holes x 20 holes
Cut 3, stitch 1

COLOR KEY
¾" Fabric Strips
☐ Yellow gold
■ Berry print
■ Wedgwood blue print
■ Jade print
☐ Off-white with small Wedgwood
   blue pattern
╱ Berry print Straight Stitch

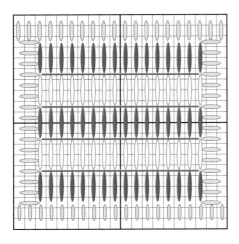

Centerpiece Box Short Side
20 holes x 20 holes
Cut 2

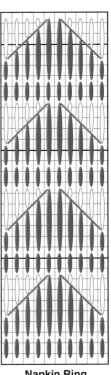

Napkin Ring
10 holes x 33 holes
Cut 1

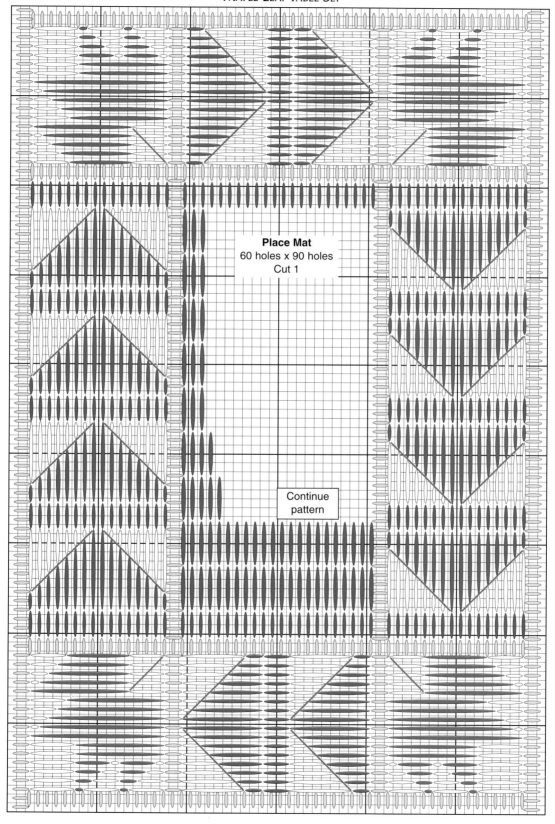

Place Mat
60 holes x 90 holes
Cut 1

Continue
pattern

Chapter Two

LIVING IN STYLE

Add warm and cozy touches to your home's entrance, and liing and family rooms by including attractive craft projects in your decor. Projects such as a cheerful welcome wreath and house number signs will give your homne a hosp8itable feel, while a handsome backgammon board will provide the evening's activities.

BACKGAMMON SET

Enjoy a challenging game of backgammon played with
this complete set including backgammon board,
game pieces and box for holding playing pieces.

Skill Level: Advanced beginner

Materials
- 3 sheets 7-count stiff plastic canvas
- Worsted weight yarn as listed in color key
- Game pieces (checkers)
- Pair of dice
- Hot-glue gun

Instructions

1. Cut plastic canvas according to graphs (pages 38–40). Cut two 32-hole x 6-hole pieces for box long sides, two 20-hole x 6-hole pieces for box short sides, two 18-hole x 5-hole pieces for short spacer and two 22-hole x 5-hole pieces for long spacer.

2. Stitch pieces following graphs. For Woven Band Stitches (Fig. 1) on game board and box lid top, use light berry and Windsor blue. Continental Stitch box sides and spacers with eggshell.

3. Work Backstitches on game board pieces, lid sides and dice cup sides over completed background stitching.

4. Overcast edges of box bottom, top edges of dice cup sides and corners and bottom edges of lid sides with claret. Overcast top edges of box sides with eggshell.

5. Using claret through step 6, Overcast top, bottom and left sides of both game board pieces. With right sides up, lay board pieces with unstitched edges side by side. Whipstitch these edges together.

6. Whipstitch four dice cup sides to four dice cup corners, then Whipstitch these sides and corners to one cup bottom. Repeat with remaining cup pieces. Whip stitch lid sides together, then Whipstitch sides to top.

Fig. 1

Bring needle up at 1, down at 2, up at 3, down at 4, etc., completing numbered stitching with Windsor blue. With light berry, bring needle up at A, down at B, up at C, down at D, etc., weaving through Windsor blue stitches as shown, until border is completed.

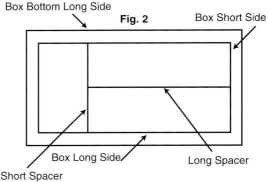

Fig. 2

Box Bottom Long Side
Box Short Side
Box Long Side
Long Spacer
Short Spacer

7. Using eggshell through step 8, stitch box sides to box bottom where indicated on graph, then Whipstitch sides together.

8. With wrong sides of piece together, Whipstitch short spacers together along all four sides and long spacers together along all four sides. Glue spacers inside box to box bottom, sides and each other (see Fig.2).

9. Place game pieces and dice in box.

—Designed by Celia Lange Designs

BACKGAMMON SET

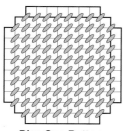

Dice Cup Bottom
11 holes x 11 holes
Cut 2

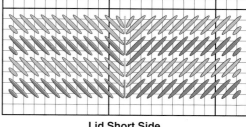

Lid Short Side
23 holes x 11 holes
Cut 2

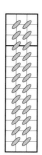

Dice Cup Corner
3 holes x 13 holes
Cut 8

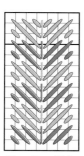

Dice Cup Side
7 holes x 13 holes
Cut 8

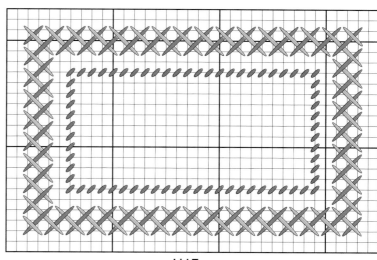

Lid Top
35 holes x 23 holes
Cut 1

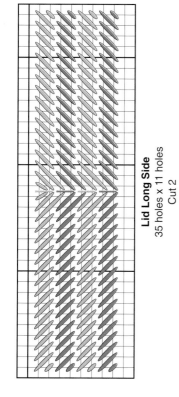

Lid Long Side
35 holes x 11 holes
Cut 2

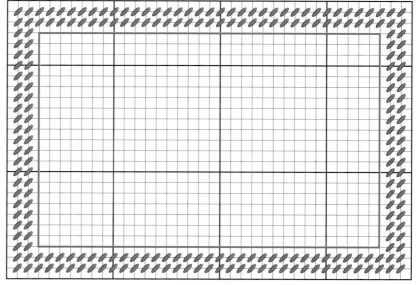

Box Bottom
38 holes x 26 holes
Cut 1

BACKGAMMON SET

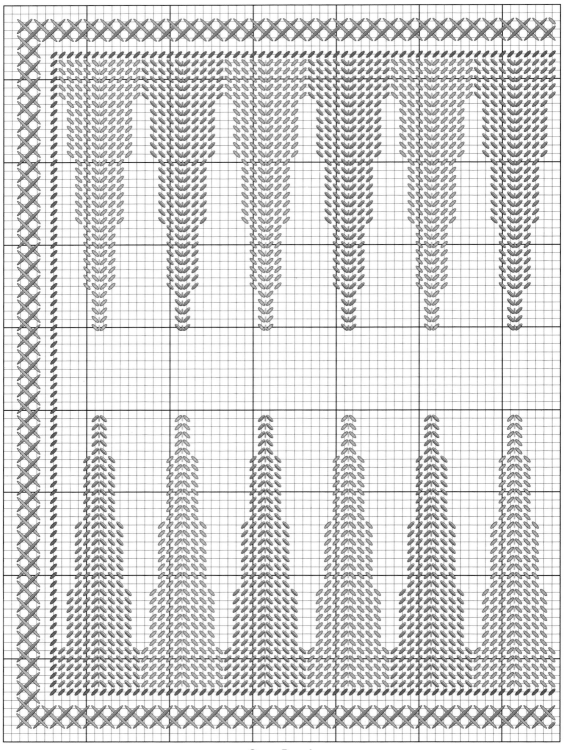

Game Board
67 holes x 89 holes
Cut 2

IVY HOUSE SIGN

Give the entrance to your home an added accent with this attractive house number sign. It's pretty as well as practical.

Skill Level: Beginner

Materials
- 1 artist-size sheet 7-count plastic canvas
- Worsted weight yarn as listed in color key
- #16 tapestry needle
- 14" x 10" piece cardboard
- Sawtooth hanger
- Hot-glue gun

Instructions

1. Cut plastic canvas according to graph (page 42).

2. Using numbers provided, center and Continental Stitch numbers with medium damson between yellow lines on graph, allowing three bars between numbers. Larger numbers may need to have fewer bars between numbers.

3. Stitch border following graph. Fill in background behind numbers with natural, repeating pattern of vertical rows of Slanting Gobelin over two bars, then Continental Stitches. Overcast edges with damson.

4. Cut cardboard to fit; glue to backside of stitched piece. Glue hanger to center top back of cardboard.

—Designed by Joan Green

COLOR KEY

Worsted Weight Yarn	Yards
Light damson #8854	12
Medium damson #8855	10
Light sea green #8878	10
Pale sea green #8879	8
Natural #8940	52
Uncoded areas are natural #8940 Continental Stitches	
Damson #8996 Overcasting	5

Color numbers given are for Spinrite Bernat Berella "4" worsted weight yarn.

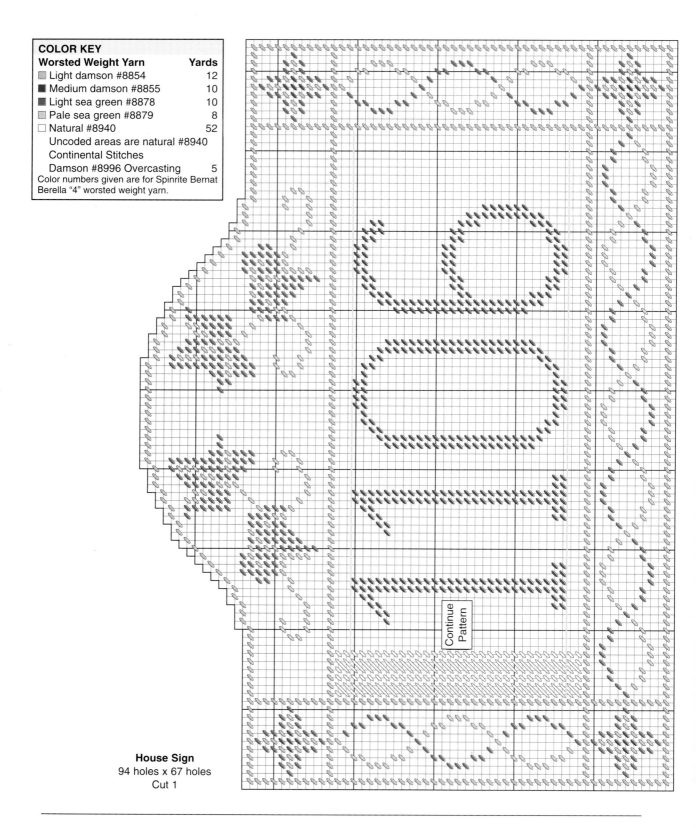

Continue Pattern

House Sign
94 holes x 67 holes
Cut 1

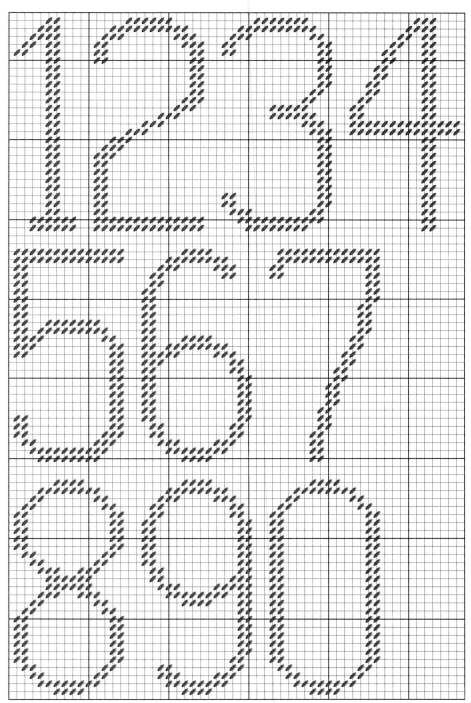

House Sign Numbers

Nut Basket Graphs

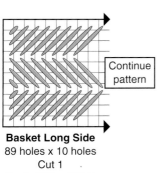

Basket Long Side
89 holes x 10 holes
Cut 1

Basket Short Side
33 holes x 10 holes
Cut 1

Arm
17 holes x 12 holes
Cut 2, reverse 1 for coaster set
Cut 2, reverse 1 for nut basket

COLOR KEY

Plastic Canvas Yarn	Yards
☐ Taupe #0020	15
■ Black #0028	2
▨ Walnut #0047	15
☐ Sand #0049	10
▨ Poplar #0051	46
Uncoded areas are curry #0014	
Continental Stitches	50
#3 Pearl Cotton	
╱ White Backstitch	2
╱ Black #310 Backstitch	4
╱ Attach coaster box	

Color numbers given are for Spinrite plastic canvas yarn and DMC #3 pearl cotton.

NUT BASKET SET

Delight family and guests with this delightful nut caddy and coaster set.
The caddy is designed to hold a nutcracker and pick, too!

Skill Level: Intermediate

Materials
- 3 sheets 7-count plastic canvas
- 6" plastic canvas radial circle
- Plastic canvas yarn as listed in color key
- #3 pearl cotton as listed in color key
- Green craft foam to match yarn
- Hot-glue gun

COASTER SET

1. Cut plastic canvas according to graphs (pages 44–46). Cut one 24-hole x 7-hole piece for coaster box bottom and two 7-hole x 3-hole pieces for coaster box sides.

2. Stitch pieces following graphs, reversing one arm before stitching. With curry, Continental Stitch basket bottom and basket sides. Do not work embroidery at this time.

3. Overcast head, body front, body back, arms and top edges of box sides with curry. Overcast small acorn and coasters from dot to dot with walnut and remaining edges with curry.

4. Backstitch with white and black pearl cotton following graphs.

5. With curry, Whipstitch bottom edges of box sides to short edges of box bottom. Glue box to body front and back where indicated on graphs.

6. Using photo as a guide, glue head to top of body front. Glue small acorn to center of body front, then glue arms to body front and acorn with paws over acorn.

7. Place acorn coasters upside down in box so they do not show behind body front.

NUT BASKET

1. Cut plastic canvas according to graphs (pages 44– 46).

2. Stitch pieces following graphs, reversing one arm before stitching. Do not work embroidery at this time. Radial circle will remain unstitched.

3. Overcast head, body front, body back and arms with curry. Overcast small acorn from dot to dot with walnut and remaining edges with curry.

4. Backstitch with white and black pearl cotton following graphs.

5. Using poplar through step 6, Whipstitch basket sides together, forming a circle. Overcast top edge of basket side.

6. Using basket side and radial circle (basket bottom) as templates, cut craft foam to fit. Whipstitch outside edge of circle to bottom edge of basket side.

7. Trimming as necessary to fit, glue craft foam inside basket to sides and bottom, placing craft foam seam in middle of small side section.

8. Using photo as a guide through step 9, glue head to top of body front. Glue squirrel front to inside of basket, centered between two side seams. Glue squirrel back to outside of basket and to body front.

9. Glue shoulders of arms to body front. Glue small acorn behind front paws, leaving a space between body and paws.

—Designed by Celia Lange Designs

Small Acorn
8 holes x 8 holes
Cut 1 for coaster set
Cut 1 for nut basket

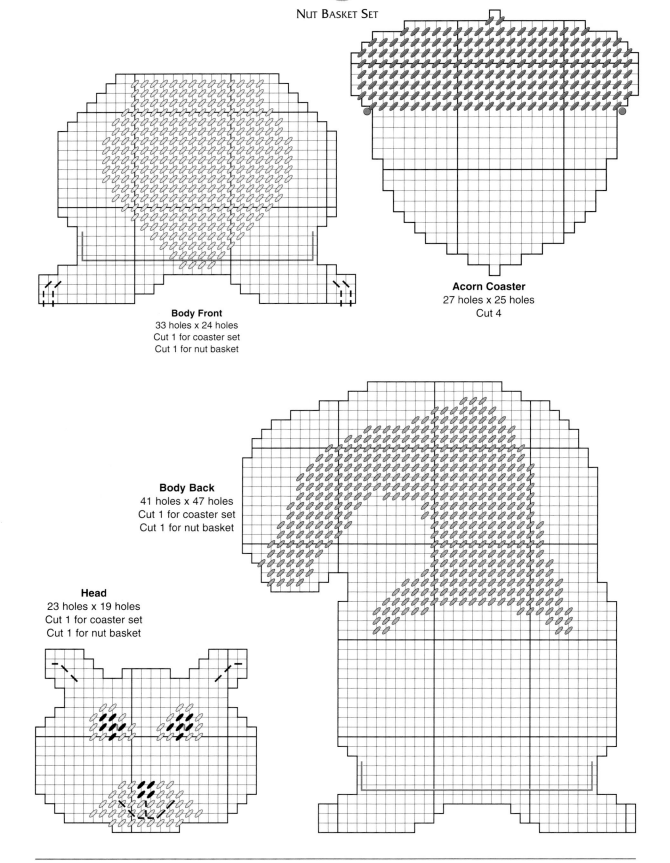

Body Front
33 holes x 24 holes
Cut 1 for coaster set
Cut 1 for nut basket

Acorn Coaster
27 holes x 25 holes
Cut 4

Body Back
41 holes x 47 holes
Cut 1 for coaster set
Cut 1 for nut basket

Head
23 holes x 19 holes
Cut 1 for coaster set
Cut 1 for nut basket

MAGAZINE HOLDER

*Keep your favorite magazines tidy and close at hand
with this attractive magazine holder. Stitch it in one
of the rich colors shown or a color to suit your decor.*

Skill Level: Beginner

Materials
- 3 sheets 7-count stiff plastic canvas
- Worsted weight yarn as listed in color key
- ⅛"-wide plastic canvas metallic yarn
- 1/16"-wide plastic canvas metallic yarn

Instructions

1. Cut plastic canvas according to graphs (below and page 49). Cut one 61-hole x 20-hole piece for holder bottom and one 20-hole x 80-hole piece for inner spine.

2. Stitch pieces with new berry following graphs. Work ⅛"-wide gold metallic yarn Smyrna Cross Stitches next. Stitch embroidery with ⅛"-wide and 1/16"-wide gold metallic yarn last.

3. Using new berry through step 5, Overcast top edge of inner spine; Continental Stitch the next two bars. Continental Stitch holder bottom piece.

4. Overcast top and bottom edges of outer spine. Whipstitch bottom edge of inner spine to one short edge of bottom piece, then Whipstitch sides of both spines to long straight edges of sides. *Note: Outer spine will bow out. Do not join outer spine to inner spine at top or bottom edges.*

5. Whipstitch sides and back to bottom piece, then Whipstitch back to sides. Overcast remaining edges.

—Designed by Celia Lange Designs

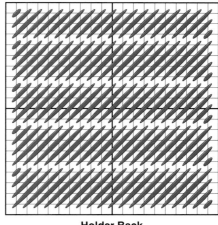

Holder Back
20 holes x 20 holes
Cut 1

Holder Outer Spine
21 holes x 80 holes
Cut 1

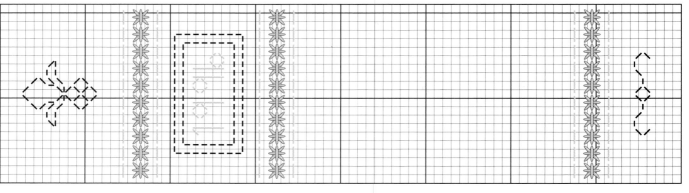

Holder Side
61 holes x 80 holes
Cut 2, reverse 1

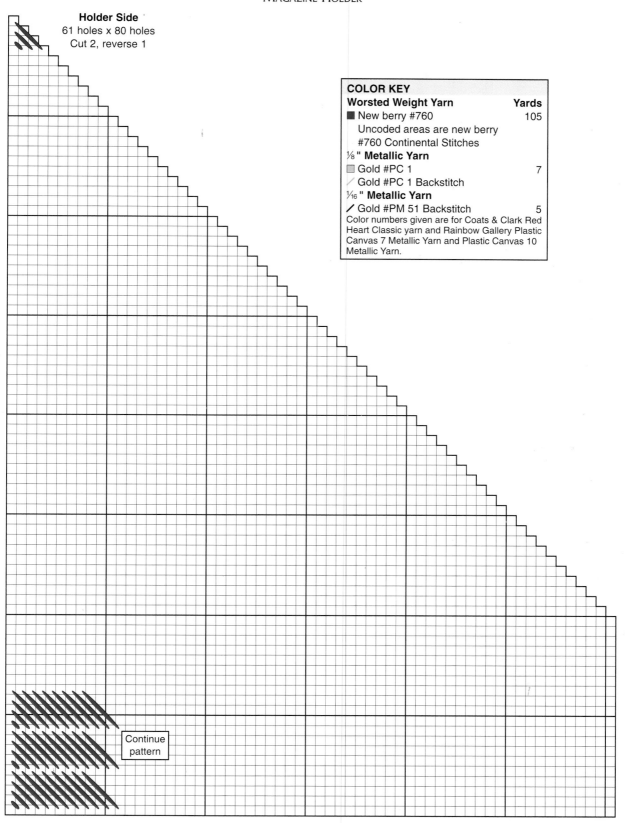

Continue pattern

COLOR KEY

Worsted Weight Yarn	Yards
■ New berry #760	105
Uncoded areas are new berry #760 Continental Stitches	
⅛ " **Metallic Yarn**	
▨ Gold #PC 1	7
╱ Gold #PC 1 Backstitch	
⅟₁₆ " **Metallic Yarn**	
╱ Gold #PM 51 Backstitch	5

Color numbers given are for Coats & Clark Red Heart Classic yarn and Rainbow Gallery Plastic Canvas 7 Metallic Yarn and Plastic Canvas 10 Metallic Yarn.

SUNFLOWER WELCOME

Stacked on top of one another or lined up in a row,
these delightful blocks are sure to win you
praise while making your guests feel at home!

Skill Level: Intermediate

Materials
- 3 sheets 14-count brown plastic canvas
- #5 pearl cotton as listed in color key
- #22 tapestry needle
- 28 (⁵⁄₁₆") white 4-hole buttons
- 9" 20-gauge white cloth stem wire

Instructions
1. Cut plastic canvas according to graphs (below). Thirty-five block squares will remain unstitched.

2. Stitch black-and-white border on seven squares. Sew on buttons with black where indicated on graph.

3. Center each letter inside border and Continental

Stitch two "E's" and one each of the letters "W," "L," "C," "O" and "M." For the letter "E", turn the "W" graph sideways and Continental Stitch from lower left hole to upper right hole. The letter "M" is the letter "W" turned upside down.

4. Divide block squares into seven sets of six squares; include one stitched square in each set. With blue, Whipstitch each set together, forming a cube.

5. Stitch flower following graph; do not Overcast.

6. Wrap one end of stem wire loosely and unevenly around pencil. Tack this end to back of flower with white. Insert remaining end of wire into any hole on top of any block (see photo).

—Designed by Kathy Wirth

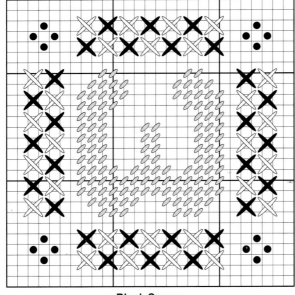

Block Square
27 holes x 27 holes
Cut 42, stitch 7
See instructions before stitching

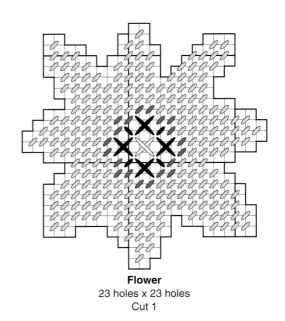

Flower
23 holes x 23 holes
Cut 1

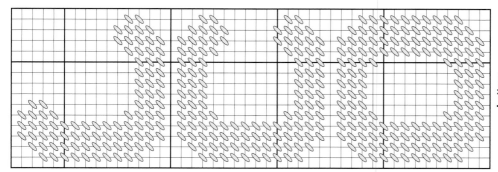

Letters

COLOR KEY	
#5 Pearl Cotton	**Yards**
☐ White	7
■ Black #310	8
☐ Bright canary #973	11
▨ Imperial blue #995	23
● Attach button	
Color numbers given are for DMC #5 pearl cotton.	

CHEERFUL PLANT POKES

Tucked into a lush green plant, each of these delightful pokes will add just the right splash of color all year long!

Skill Level: Beginner

BIRDHOUSE

Materials
- ¼ sheet 7-count plastic canvas
- Plastic canvas yarn as listed in color key
- #16 tapestry needle
- 1 yard blue satin raffia ribbon
- 6 satin ribbon roses in assorted pastel colors
- Small mushroom bird
- 1½"-long craft pick
- Jumbo craft stick
- Low-temperature glue gun

Instructions
1. Cut plastic canvas according to graph (page 53).

2. Stitch birdhouse following graph. Overcast with white.

3. For perch, glue craft pick to birdhouse where indicated on graph. Glue bird to pick. Using photo as a guide, glue five roses to left side of house.

4. Cut raffia ribbon into three equal lengths. Tie three lengths together in a bow; curl tails. Glue bow under perch, then glue remaining rose to center of bow.

5. Center and glue jumbo craft stick to backside of birdhouse.

WATERING CAN

Materials
- ¼ sheet 7-count plastic canvas
- Plastic canvas yarn as listed in color key
- #16 tapestry needle
- 2 yards cranberry satin raffia ribbon
- Small mushroom bird
- Jumbo craft stick
- Low-temperature glue gun

Instructions
1. Cut plastic canvas according to graph (below).

2. Stitch watering can following graph. Overcast around top from dot to dot with baby green. Overcast remaining edges with lavender.

3. Cut raffia ribbon into four equal lengths. Tie four lengths together in a bow; curl tails. Center and glue bow approximately three or four bars from bottom edge. Glue bird to center of bow.

4. Center and glue jumbo craft stick to backside of watering can.

—Designed by Adele Mogavero

Watering Can
36 holes x 35 holes
Cut 1

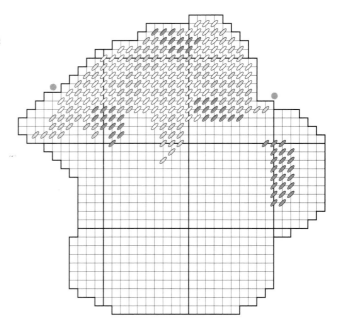

Birdhouse
27 holes x 31 holes
Cut 1

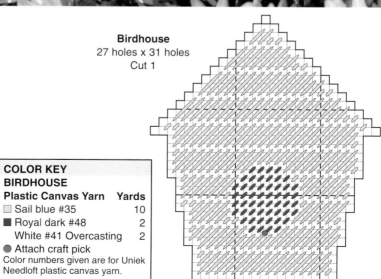

COLOR KEY
WATERING CAN

Plastic Canvas Yarn	Yards
☐ Straw #19	2
▨ Mint #24	2
☐ Moss #25	2
☐ Baby green #26	2
▨ Eggshell #39	2
☐ White #41	3
Uncoded areas are lavender #05	
Continental Stitches	15

Color numbers given are for Uniek Needloft plastic canvas yarn.

COLOR KEY
BIRDHOUSE

Plastic Canvas Yarn	Yards
☐ Sail blue #35	10
■ Royal dark #48	2
White #41 Overcasting	2
● Attach craft pick	

Color numbers given are for Uniek Needloft plastic canvas yarn.

QUILT COASTERS

*Stitch this eye-catching coaster set to use when serving
up mugs of steaming hot apple cider in the winter or
tall, cool glasses of lemonade in the summer!*

Skill Level: Intermediate

Materials
- 3 sheets 10-count black plastic canvas
- #3 pearl cotton as listed in color key
- 6-strand black embroidery floss
- #20 tapestry needle
- 1½ sheets black adhesive-backed felt

COASTER BOX

1. Cut plastic canvas according to graphs (pages 55 and 56). Cut four 39-hole x 24-hole pieces for box liner. Box bottom and liner pieces will remain unstitched.

2. Stitch pieces following graphs, beginning with the light peach and light blue. Try not to carry stitches across open areas.

3. With light blue, Whipstitch right edges of lid sides A to left edges of lid sides B. Whipstitch two remaining lid sides together with light peach.

4. Whipstitch top edges of lid sides A to sides A of lid top with light peach. Whipstitch top edges of lid sides B to sides B of lid top with light blue.

5. Following instructions for steps 3 and 4, Whipstitch box sides A and B together then Whipstitch

bottom edges of box sides to box bottom. *Note: Remaining edges of box and lid are not Overcast.*

6. Cut two 4" squares of black felt. Apply one to inside of lid top and one to bottom inside box.

7. Using black floss throughout, Whipstitch short edges of liner pieces together. Insert liner into box. Tack liner to top edges of box and corners.

COASTERS

1. Cut 12 coasters according to graph (page 56). Six pieces liners will remain unstitched.

2. Stitch six pieces following main pattern on graph, beginning with the lightest colors. Try not to carry stitches across open areas. Do not yet work the outer row of stitches.

3. Place one liner under each stitched coaster. Work outer row of stitches through both coaster and liner using a different color of pearl cotton for each coaster.

4. Using coasters as templates, cut felt slightly smaller than coasters. Apply felt to back of each coaster.

—Designed by Kathy Wirth

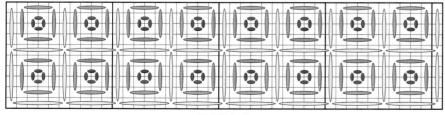

Lid Side A
41 holes x 10 holes
Cut 2

COLOR KEY	
#3 Pearl Cotton	**Skeins**
☐ Light peach #8	2
▨ Medium peach #10	2
■ Dark peach #13	2
▨ Medium blue #167	2
■ Dark blue #169	2
☐ Light blue #847	2
Color numbers given are for Coats & Clark Anchor #3 pearl cotton.	

Lid Side B
41 holes x 10 holes
Cut 2

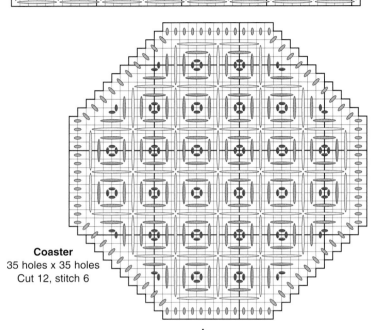

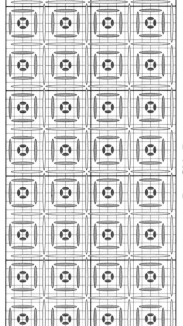

Box Side B
41 holes x 20 holes
Cut 2

Coaster
35 holes x 35 holes
Cut 12, stitch 6

A

Box Side A
41 holes x 20 holes
Cut 2

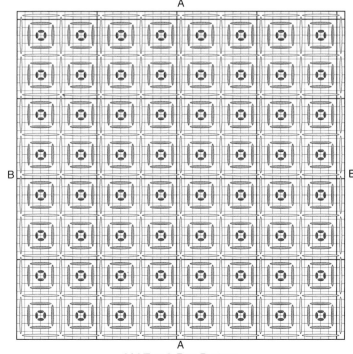

B

B

A

Lid Top & Box Bottom
41 holes x 41 holes
Cut 2, stitch 1

BLESS OUR HOME

Stitch this country-style sign to display in your home.
It makes an extra-special house-warming gift too!

Skill Level: Beginner

Materials

- 1 sheet 7-count plastic canvas
- Worsted weight yarn as listed in color key
- #16 tapestry needle
- 13½" x 5¾" piece cardboard
- Sawtooth hanger

Instructions

1. Cut plastic canvas according to graph (page 58).

2. Stitch plastic canvas following graph. Overcast edges with midnight.

3. Glue cardboard to backside of stitched piece. Glue sawtooth hanger to center top back of cardboard.

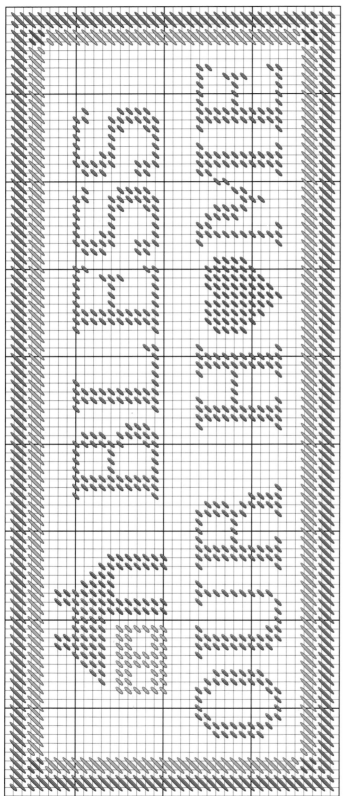

COLOR KEY

Worsted Weight Yarn	Yards
■ Midnight #8805	20
■ Cinnabar #8812	3
■ Light sea green #8878	7
Uncoded area is honey #8795	
Continental Stitches	32

Color numbers given are for Spinrite Bernat Berella "4" worsted weight yarn.

Bless Our Home
90 holes x 38 holes
Cut 1

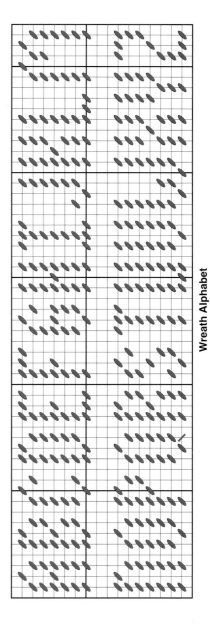

WELCOME WREATH

*Welcome friends and extended family into your
home with this charming wreath featuring
your family name and a pretty cottage.*

Skill Level: Advanced beginner

Materials
- 2 sheets 7-count plastic canvas
- Worsted weight yarn as listed in color key
- #16 tapestry needle
- 15" grapevine wreath
- 1 yard ½"-wide pink satin ribbon
- 6" x 8" piece cardboard
- Hot-glue gun

Instructions

1. Cut plastic canvas according to graphs (page 61).

2. Stitch house following graph. When background
stitching is completed, work rose French Knots
with 4 plies yarn and black Backstitches with 2
plies yarn. Overcast with adjacent colors. Tab will
remain unstitched.

3. Using house as a template, cut cardboard to fit;
glue to backside of house. *Note: Do not cover tab
area with cardboard.*

4. For welcome piece, using alphabet provided,
center and Continental Stitch letters of name between
blue lines on graph, allowing one bar between letters.
Complete stitching following graph, filling in area
behind name with pale tapestry gold Continental
Stitches. Overcast with dark Oxford heather.

5. Cut ribbon in half. With needle, thread ribbon
through hole indicated on sign graph. Weave ends
on backside of graph through grapevine; adjust so
ends are even. Tie ribbon in a bow, trimming ends
as desired. Lightly glue outer edges to wreath.

6. Using photo as a guide, center and insert tab of
house into bottom part of wreath so house stands
up in middle of wreath. Glue tab securely to wreath.

—Designed by Joan Green

Wreath Alphabet

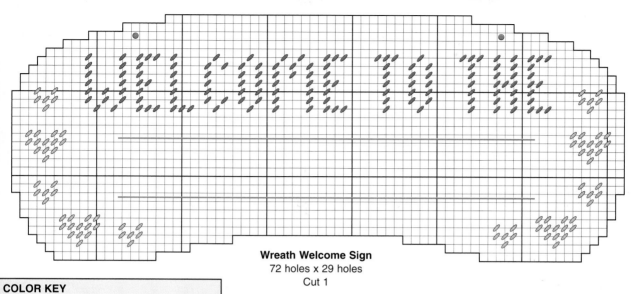

Wreath Welcome Sign
72 holes x 29 holes
Cut 1

COLOR KEY

Worsted Weight Yarn	Yards
■ Dark denim #8793	10
▨ Light antique rose #8815	5
▨ Light sea green #8878	4
□ Pale tapestry gold #8887	28
▨ Dark Oxford heather #8893	10
□ White #8942	2
■ Black #8994	2

Uncoded area is pale tapestry gold
#8887 Continental Stitches
● Light antique rose #8815
French Knot
╱ Black #8994 Backstitch
● Ribbon placement
Color numbers given are for Spinrite Bernat Berella
"4" worsted weight yarn.

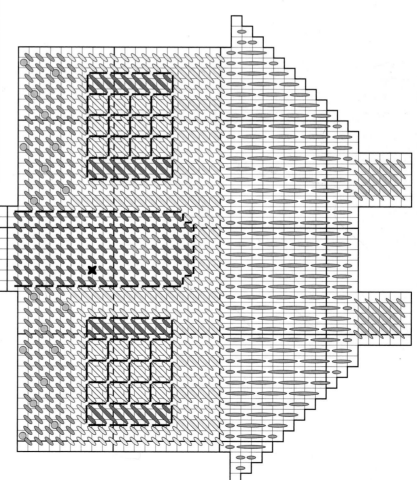

Wreath House
44 holes x 48 holes
Cut 1

Chapter Three

HOME OFFICE HELPERS

Keep your home office and hobby room in tip-top shape with the wonderful projects included in this chapter. From organizers to craft storage boxes, you'll have your home office looking great!

LODGE-LOOK DESK SET

Treat yourself to this handsome four-piece desk set.
Stitched on 7-count plastic canvas, each piece will work up
quickly and help you with all your home office activities!

Skill Level: Intermediate

Materials
- 1 artist-size sheet 7-count plastic canvas
- 4 (10½" x 13½") sheets 7-count plastic canvas
- Plastic canvas yarn as listed in color key
- Brown blotter paper

Cutting & Stitching

1. From 10½" x 13½" sheets, cut plastic canvas according to graphs (pages 64–66); cut one 19-hole x 19-hole piece for pencil box bottom, one 17-hole x 11-hole piece for covered box bottom, two 17-hole x 12-hole pieces for covered box large sides and two 11-hole x 12-hole pieces for covered box small sides.

2. Do not cut artist-size sheet, which will remain unstitched and will be used for blotter base.

3. Stitch pieces following graphs, repeating acorn and canoe motifs on blotter pockets where indicated. Continental Stitch pencil box bottom with tan. Continental Stitch covered box sides and covered box bottom with medium avocado.

Assembly

1. For desk blotter, align top, bottom and right edges of one blotter pocket with one short end of blotter base. Align top, bottom and left edges of remaining blotter pocket with remaining short end of blotter base.

2. Using brown throughout, Overcast inside edges of pockets. Whipstitch pockets and blotter base together, Overcasting remaining edges of base while Whipstitching.

3. Cut blotter paper to fit, using two or three layers as necessary for smooth writing surface. Insert paper into blotter.

4. Using brown throughout, Overcast top edges of pencil box sides. Whipstitch sides together, then Whipstitch bottom to sides.

5. Using medium avocado throughout, Overcast top edges of covered box sides. Whipstitch sides together, then Whipstitch sides to bottom.

6. With honey gold, Whipstitch covered box lid sides together. With brown, Whipstitch lid sides to lid top; Overcast bottom edges of lid sides.

7. Using brown through step 8, Overcast side and bottom edges of photo frame stand, inside edges of frame front and bottom edges of frame front and frame back.

8. Whipstitch top edge of frame stand to frame back where indicated on graph. With wrong sides together, Whipstitch frame front to frame back along top and side edges.

9. Cut a 2"–2½" length of brown yarn. Attach one end of yarn to center bottom of stand. Attach remaining end to center bottom of frame. If desired, use blotter paper for picture mat.

—Designed by Nancy Marshall

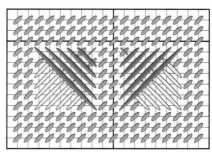

Covered Box Lid Top
19 holes x 13 holes
Cut 1

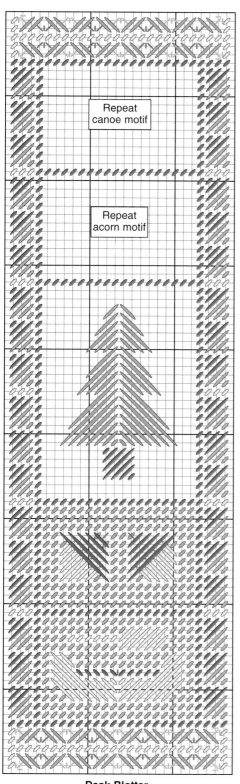

Desk Blotter
27 holes x 90 holes
Cut 2

COLOR KEY

Plastic Canvas Yarn	Yards
■ Bronze #286	16
□ Tan #334	31
■ Medium brown #337	68
□ Honey gold #645	6
■ Medium avocado #657	35
■ Blue gray #807	21

Uncoded areas are tan #334
Continental Stitches
╱ Bronze #286 Backstitch
╱ Medium brown #337 Backstitch
╱ Blue gray #807 Backstitch
╱ Whipstitch to frame stand
Color numbers given are for J. & P. Coats
plastic canvas yarn.

Covered Box Short Side
13 holes x 5 holes
Cut 2

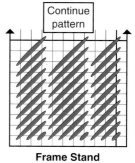

Continue pattern

Frame Stand
11 holes x 40 holes
Cut 1

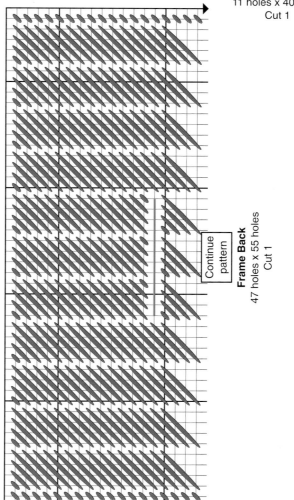

Continue pattern

Frame Back
47 holes x 55 holes
Cut 1

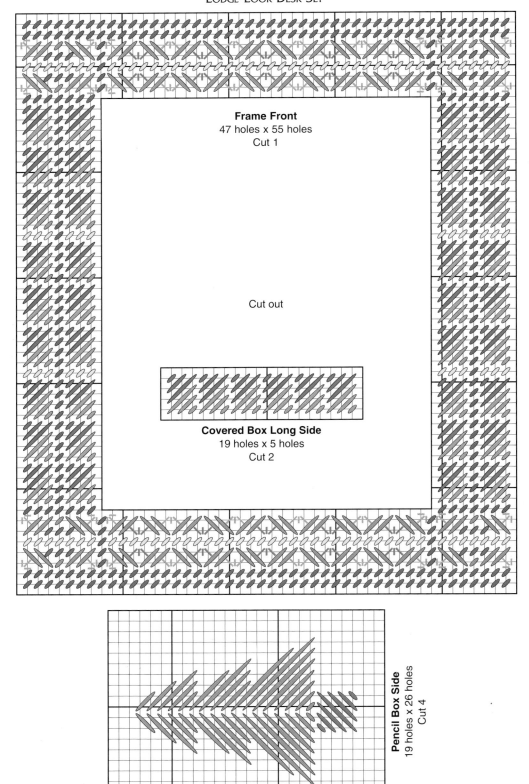

Frame Front
47 holes x 55 holes
Cut 1

Cut out

Covered Box Long Side
19 holes x 5 holes
Cut 2

Pencil Box Side
19 holes x 26 holes
Cut 4

COMPUTER DISK CADDY

Tuck your 3-inch floppy disks into this handsome caddy!
Rich blue bargello stitches make this suitable for both men and women!

Skill Level: Intermediate

Materials
- 1½ sheets 7-count stiff plastic canvas
- Worsted weight yarn as listed in color key
- #16 tapestry needle
- Felt in coordinating color (optional)
- Hot-glue gun (optional)

Instructions

1. Cut plastic canvas according to graphs (page 68). Cut one 54-hole x 30-hole piece for caddy bottom and one 54-hole x 27-hole piece for caddy back. Cut two 25-hole x 25-hole pieces for drawer backs and six 28-hole x 25-hole pieces for drawer sides and bottoms.

2. Stitch pieces following graphs. Caddy back and bottom and drawer backs, sides and bottoms will remain unstitched.

3. Using medium navy throughout, Whipstitch caddy sides to caddy top and caddy bottom, then Whipstitch sides, top and bottom to caddy back. Overcast front edges of caddy.

4. If lining is desired, cut felt smaller than caddy back and caddy bottom; glue to outside of each piece.

5. Using light navy throughout, Whipstitch one drawer front and one drawer back to two drawer side pieces, then Whipstitch drawer bottom to front, back and sides. Overcast top edges of drawer. Repeat for second drawer.

—Designed by Joan Green

Computer Disk Caddy

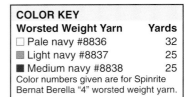

COLOR KEY

Worsted Weight Yarn	Yards
☐ Pale navy #8836	32
▨ Light navy #8837	25
■ Medium navy #8838	25

Color numbers given are for Spinrite Bernat Berella "4" worsted weight yarn.

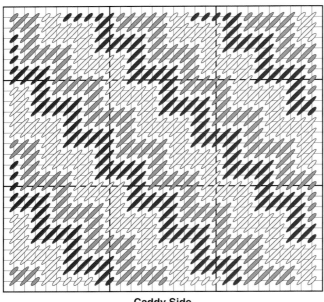

Caddy Side
30 holes x 27 holes
Cut 2

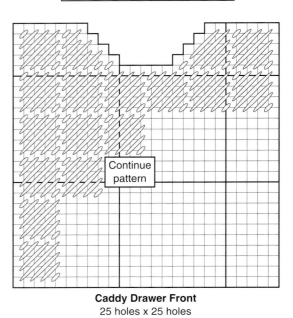

Continue pattern

Caddy Drawer Front
25 holes x 25 holes
Cut 2

Caddy Top
54 holes x 30 holes
Cut 1

Revolving Organizer

No more looking for a pen or pad of paper when you need one!
This handy organizer is easy to stitch, and will keep your
office supplies at your fingertips!

Skill Level: Beginner

Materials

- 2 sheets 7-count stiff plastic canvas
- 1 sheet 7-count regular plastic canvas
- Worsted weight yarn as listed in color key
- 10.5" x .8" white plastic turntable
- Hot-glue gun

Instructions

1. Cut four outer box sides, four inner box sides and one long divider from stiff plastic canvas according to graphs (pages 70 and 71). Cut two 20-hole x 22-hole pieces for short dividers from stiff plastic canvas. Dividers will remain unstitched.

2. Cut four turntable trim pieces from regular plastic canvas according to graph (page 71).

3. Stitch pieces following graphs. Backstitch with claret over completed background stitching.

4. Overcast top edges of all sides and dividers with white. Overcast bottom edges of all sides with light berry. With light berry, Whipstitch one side of one short divider to one of the bars indicated on the long divider graph; Whipstitch remaining short divider to opposite side of plastic canvas at second bar indicated on graph. ***Note: Divider will be in the shape of an X.***

5. Using white throughout, Whipstitch outer sides together. Whipstitch two inner sides and one divider edge together, making sure bottom edges of divider and sides are even. Repeat with remaining inner sides and divider until all four sides are Whipstitched together. ***Note: Inner box should be divided into four triangular sections.***

6. Whipstitch sides of turntable trim pieces together with claret, then Overcast top and bottom edges with white.

7. Using photo as a guide through step 8, center and glue trim to outer edge of turntable. Fit will be snug.

8. Center and glue outer box to turntable top. Place inner box inside outer box so inner box corners are at the center of the outer box sides; glue in place.

—Designed by Celia Lange Designs

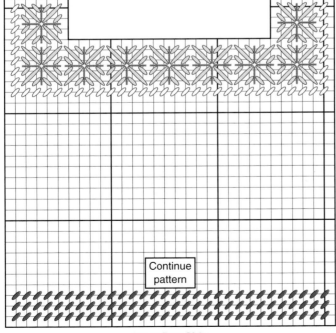

Inner Box Side
31 holes x 31 holes
Cut 4 from stiff

Continue pattern

COLOR KEY

Worsted Weight Yarn	Yards
☐ White #1	20
☐ Cameo rose #759	10
■ Light berry #761	65
╱ Claret #762 Backstitch	10
╱ Whipstitch to short divider	

Color numbers given are for Coats & Clark Red Heart Classic yarn.

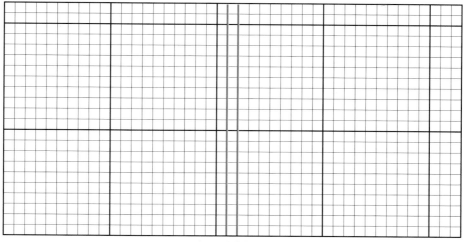

Long Divider
43 holes x 22 holes
Cut 1 from stiff

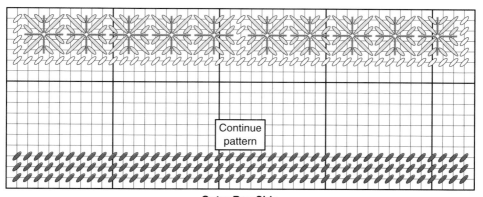

Continue
pattern

Outer Box Side
44 holes x 17 holes
Cut 4 from stiff

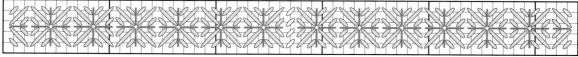

Turntable Trim
54 holes x 5 holes
Cut 4 from regular

OCTAGONAL QUILT BOX

Store spools of thread, needles and small scissors in this pretty storage box.
With its vibrant colors and eye-catching design, it will always be easy to find!

Skill Level: Advanced beginner

Materials

- 1 sheet 7-count stiff plastic canvas
- Worsted weight yarn as listed in color key
- #16 tapestry needle
- Ceramic tulip basket button #86036
- Sewing needle and matching green thread

Instructions

1. Cut plastic canvas according to graphs (pages 73 and 74). Box bottom will remain unstitched.

2. Stitch pieces following graphs. Overcast bottom edges of lid sides with natural and top edges of box sides with medium damson.

3. Using medium damson throughout, Whipstitch box sides together, stitching short sides in between large sides. Whipstitch sides to bottom.

4. Using natural throughout, Whipstitch lid sides together, stitching short sides in between long sides. Whipstitch sides to lid top.

5. With sewing needle and green thread, sew button to lid top where indicated on graph.

—Designed by Joan Green

OCTAGONAL QUILT BOX

Lid Top
47 holes x 47 holes
Cut 1

COLOR KEY	
Worsted Weight Yarn	**Yards**
☐ Natural #8940	22
▨ Medium damson #8855	40
☐ Pale sea green #8879	18
● Attach button	
Color numbers given are for Spinrite Bernat Berella "4" worsted weight yarn.	

Lid Short Side
17 Holes x 4 Holes
Cut 4

Lid Long Side
23 holes x 4 holes
Cut 4

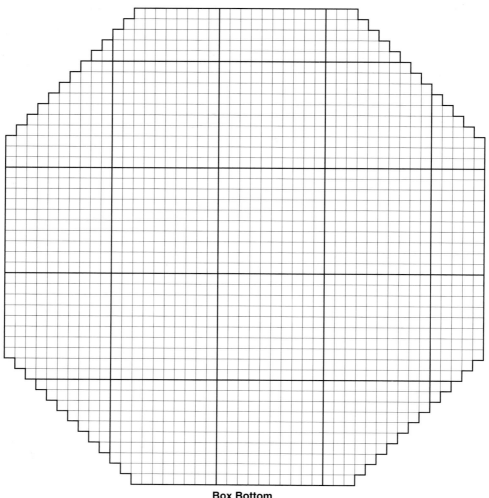

Box Bottom
45 holes x 45 holes
Cut 1
Do not stitch

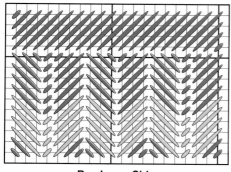

Box Large Side
21 holes x 15 holes
Cut 4

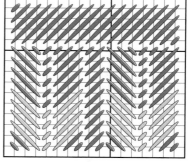

Box Short Side
17 holes x 15 holes
Cut 4

COUPON KEEPERS

*Here are two helpers sure to save you time both at home
and while shopping. A handy coupon box will keep your coupons
organized while a smaller carrier is perfect for trips to the store!*

Skill Level: Beginner

Materials
- 2 sheets 7-count plastic canvas
- Plastic canvas yarn as listed in color key
- 6-strand embroidery floss
- #16 and #18 tapestry needles
- 4" x 6" index guide cards

Instructions

1. Cut plastic canvas according to graphs (pages 76 and 77). Cut one 42-hole x 26-hole piece for box bottom, two 42-hole x 13-hole pieces for carrier pockets and one 42-hole x 2-hole piece for carrier spine. Box bottom and carrier pockets will remain unstitched.

2. Continental Stitch pieces following graphs.

Continental Stitch spine with eggshell. With 12 strands floss, work embroidery over completed background stitching.

3. Using eggshell through step 5, Overcast bottom edges of lid sides and top edges of box front, back and sides. Whipstitch box front, back and sides together, then front, back and sides to box bottom. Whipstitch lid sides together, then lid sides to lid top.

4. For coupon carrier, Whipstitch top edges of front and back to long edges of spine.

5. Align carrier pocket edges with bottom and side edges of front and back pieces on wrong side of carrier. Whipstitch together, Overcasting remaining edges of carrier while Whipstitching.

—Designed by Angie Arickx

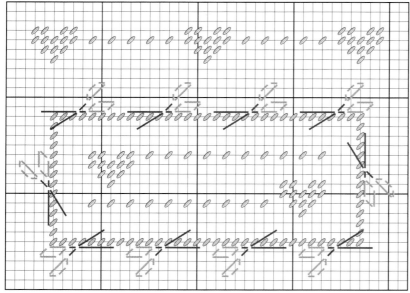

Organizer Box Front & Back
42 holes x 30 holes
Cut 2

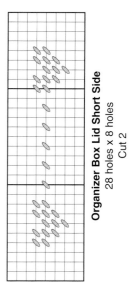

Organizer Box Lid Short Side
28 holes x 8 holes
Cut 2

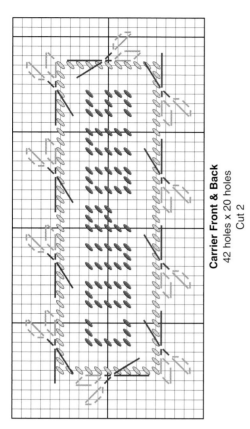

Carrier Front & Back
42 holes x 20 holes
Cut 2

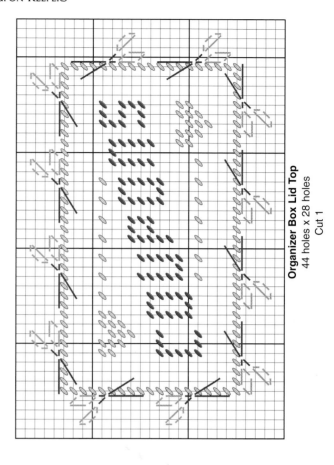

Organizer Box Lid Top
44 holes x 28 holes
Cut 1

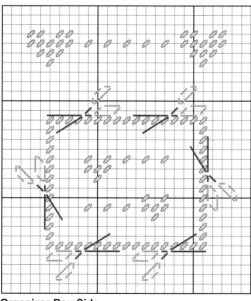

Organizer Box Side
26 holes x 30 holes
Cut 2

COLOR KEY	
Plastic Canvas Yarn	**Yards**
▨ Lavender #05	10
■ Teal #50	4
▨ Aqua #51	11
Uncoded areas are eggshell #39	
Continental Stitches	129
6-Strand Embroidery Floss	
╱ Dark pewter gray #413 Backstitch	22
╱ Medium dark antique mauve	
#3726 Backstitch	26

Color numbers given are for Uniek Needloft plastic
canvas yarn and DMC 6-strand embroidery floss.

Organizer Box Lid Long Side
44 holes x 8 holes
Cut 2

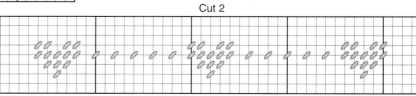

ARTS MAGNET COLLECTION

*Keep those important messages and reminders on the side
of your filing cabinet with this set of artistic magnets!*

Skill Level: Beginner

Materials

All Projects
- Small piece 7-count plastic canvas
- Worsted weight yarn as listed in color key
- Magnet strip or round magnet
- Hot-glue gun

Ballet Slippers
- 1 yard ¼"-wide medium pink ribbon

Chef's Hat
- ½ yard red #3 pearl cotton

Comedy & Tragedy
- 1 yard black #3 pearl cotton
- 2 (½") pale pink pompons
- 30" ⅛"-wide bright pink satin ribbon
- 5mm crystal round faceted stone

Director's Slate
- 2½" silver star appliqué

Guitar
- #3 pearl cotton:
  2 yards ecru
  1 yard black
- Toothpick

Palette
- 4¼" eye shadow brush
- Green acrylic craft paint

Quill
- ⅛"-wide plastic canvas metallic yarn as listed in color key
- Toothpick
- Gold metallic craft paint

Stage Bill
- ⅛"-wide plastic canvas metallic yarn as listed in color key
- 1½ yards black #3 pearl cotton

Treble Clef Sign
- 1 yard black #3 pearl cotton

BALLET SLIPPERS

1. Cut plastic canvas according to graphs (page 80).

2. Continental Stitch pieces following graphs. Work Turkey Loops with grenadine. Overcast toes of slippers and portion of slipper A from black dot to black dot with new berry. Overcast circle and remaining edges of slippers with grenadine.

3. Cut two 4½" lengths and one 6" length from medium pink ribbon. Thread the two 4½" lengths from back to front on slipper B at blue dots. Pull ribbon through until a ½" end remains. Glue ends to backside of slipper. Glue remaining ends to circle front.

4. Thread the 6" length through hole on slipper A at blue dot and pull through to center of ribbon. Glue ribbon behind slipper to backside. Glue ends to circle front, placing slipper A to the left of slipper B.

5. Using photo as a guide, glue left ribbon of slipper B to front of slipper, then glue slipper A to left ribbon of slipper B above slipper B.

6. Cut remaining ribbon into three equal lengths; tie each in a bow. Glue bows on top of each other on circle front.

7. Glue magnet to backside of circle.

CHEF'S HAT

1. Cut plastic canvas according to graph (page 80).

2. Continental Stitch hat following graph. Backstitch letters with red pearl cotton. Overcast with light periwinkle.

3. Glue magnet strip or round magnet to backside.

COMEDY & TRAGEDY

1. Cut plastic canvas according to graphs (page 81).

2. Continental Stitch masks following graphs. Add black pearl cotton Straight Stitches over completed background stitching. Overcast top portion of masks from dot to dot with black yarn. Overcast remaining edges with white yarn.

3. Cut bright pink ribbon into four 7½" lengths. On both sides of each mask, attach pink ribbon just under top points on backside. Curl ribbon with a flat straight edge.

4. Glue one pompon to each mask where indicated on graphs. Glue faceted stone to tragedy where indicated on graph.

5. Glue magnet strip or round magnet to backside of each piece.

DIRECTOR'S SLATE

1. Cut plastic canvas according to graphs (page 81).

2. Stitch pieces following graphs. Overcast top edge of slate bottom and all edges of slate top following graphs. Overcast remaining edges of bottom with black.

3. Glue star appliqué where indicated on graph. Using photo as a guide, glue lower left edge of slate top behind upper left edge of slate bottom.

4. Glue magnet strip or round magnet to backside of slate bottom.

GUITAR

1. Cut plastic canvas according to graph (page 82).

2. Stitch guitar following graph. Do not work embroidery at this time. Overcast neck with black yarn and remaining edges with bronze yarn.

3. Work black yarn French Knots and black pearl cotton Straight Stitches and French Knots. Add ecru pearl cotton Straight Stitches, then black yarn Straight Stitches.

4. For added support, glue toothpick to back of guitar neck. Glue magnet strip or round magnet to back of guitar.

PALETTE

1. Cut plastic canvas according to graph (page 81).

2. Continental Stitch palette following graph. Overcast inside and outside edges with warm brown.

3. Dip bristles of brush in green craft paint. Allow to dry. Using photo as a guide, insert handle of brush into cutout hole from front to back so approximately ½" of tip shows below bottom edge. Glue brush to palette.

4. Glue magnet to backside of palette.

QUILL

1. Cut plastic canvas according to graph (page 82).

2. Stitch piece following graph. Overcast quill portion with gold and feather with warm brown.

3. Paint approximately ½" of one tip on toothpick with gold metallic paint. Allow to dry. Glue toothpick behind quill, allowing painted tip to show below bottom edge.

4. Glue magnet strip or round magnet to backside of quill.

STAGE BILL

1. Cut plastic canvas according to graph (page 82).

2. Continental Stitch piece following graph. Add embroidery over completed background stitching. Overcast with white.

3. Glue magnet strip or round magnet to backside of stitched piece.

TREBLE CLEF SIGN

1. Cut plastic canvas according to graph (page 82).

2. Continental Stitch piece following graph. Add black pearl cotton Straight Stitches over completed background stitching. Overcast with white.

3. Glue magnet strip or round magnet to backside of stitched piece.

—*Designed by Conn Baker Gibney*

Circle
5 holes x 5 holes
Cut 1

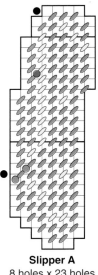

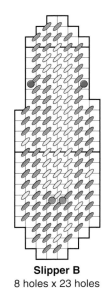

Slipper A	**Slipper B**
8 holes x 23 holes	8 holes x 23 holes
Cut 1	Cut 1

COLOR KEY
BALLET SLIPPERS

Worsted Weight Yarn	Yards
☐ Pale rose #755	1
◼ Grenadine #730	4
◼ New berry #760	2
● Grenadine #730 Turkey Loop	

Color numbers given are for Coats & Clark
Red Heart Classic yarn.

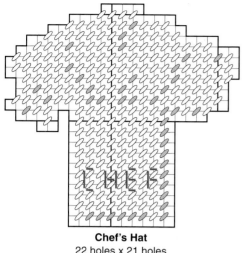

Chef's Hat
22 holes x 21 holes
Cut 1

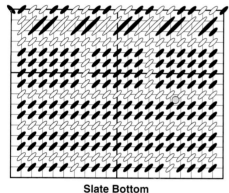

Slate Bottom
20 holes x 16 holes
Cut 1

Slate Top
20 holes x 3 holes
Cut 1

ARTS MAGNET COLLECTION

COLOR KEY
CHEF'S HAT

Worsted Weight Yarn	Yards
☐ White #1	3
▦ Light periwinkle #827	2
#3 Pearl Cotton	
╱ Red Backstitch	½

Color numbers given are for Coats & Clark
Red Heart Classic yarn.

COLOR KEY
COMEDY & TRAGEDY

Worsted Weight Yarn	Yards
☐ White #1	7
■ Black #12	2
☐ Sea coral #246	1
▦ Mist green #681	1
▦ Grenadine #730	1
#3 Pearl Cotton	
╱ Black Straight Stitch	1
⬤ Attach pompon	
⬤ Attach 5mm crystal stone	

Color numbers given are for Coats & Clark
Red Heart Classic yarn.

COLOR KEY
DIRECTOR'S SLATE

Worsted Weight Yarn	Yards
☐ White #1	3
■ Black #12	5
⬤ Attach star appliqué	

Color numbers given are for Coats & Clark
Red Heart Classic yarn.

COLOR KEY
PALETTE

Worsted Weight Yarn	Yards
☐ White #1	½
■ Black #12	½
☐ Yellow #230	½
▦ Medium coral #252	½
■ Peacock green #508	½
▦ Light lavender #579	½
■ Amethyst #588	½
■ Skipper blue #848	½
■ Jockey red #902	½
Uncoded area is warm brown #336 Continental Stitches	4

Color numbers given are for Coats & Clark
Red Heart Classic yarn.

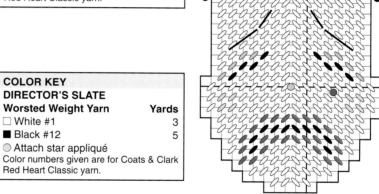

Comedy
17 holes x 21 holes
Cut 1

Tragedy
17 holes x 21 holes
Cut 1

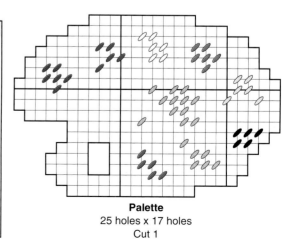

Palette
25 holes x 17 holes
Cut 1

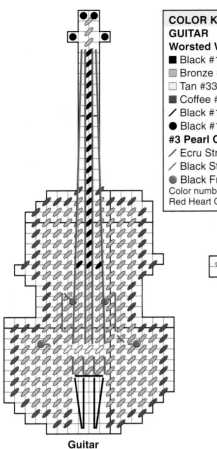

COLOR KEY
GUITAR

Worsted Weight Yarn		Yards
■	Black #12	2
▨	Bronze #286	4
☐	Tan #334	1
▨	Coffee #365	1
╱	Black #12 Straight Stitch	
●	Black #12 French Knot	

#3 Pearl Cotton

╱	Ecru Straight Stitch	2
╱	Black Straight Stitch	1
●	Black French Knot	

Color numbers given are for Coats & Clark Red Heart Classic yarn.

COLOR KEY
QUILL

Worsted Weight Yarn		Yards
■	Black #12	1
▨	Warm brown #336	3
☐	Tan #334	1

Plastic Canvas Metallic Yarn

▨	Gold PC 1	½

Color numbers given are for Coats & Clark Red Heart Classic yarn and Rainbow Gallery Plastic Canvas 7 Metallic Yarn.

Guitar
16 holes x 40 holes
Cut 1

Quill
39 holes x 14 holes
Cut 1

Stage Bill
17 holes x 23 holes
Cut 1

COLOR KEY
STAGE BILL

Worsted Weight Yarn		Yards
☐	White #1	2
▨	Yellow #230	1
■	Amethyst #588	1
	Uncoded area is jockey red #902 Continental Stitches	4

Plastic Canvas Metallic Yarn

▨	Gold PC 1	1
╱	Gold PC 1 Straight Stitch	
●	Gold PC 1 French Knot	

#3 Pearl Cotton

╱	Black Backstitch	

Color numbers given are for Coats & Clark Red Heart Classic Yarn and Rainbow Gallery Plastic Canvas 7 Metallic Yarn.

COLOR KEY
TREBLE CLEF SIGN

Worsted Weight Yarn		Yards
☐	White #1	4
■	Black #12	2

#3 Pearl Cotton

╱	Black Straight Stitch	1

Color numbers given are for Coats & Clark Red Heart Classic yarn.

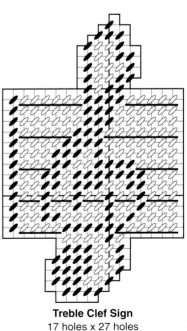

Treble Clef Sign
17 holes x 27 holes
Cut 1

I LOVE CRAFTS

This charming basket serves double duty as a unique decoration and as a useful storage basket for plastic canvas cutters and frequently used skeins of yarn!

Skill Level: Beginner

Materials
- 2 sheets 7-count plastic canvas
- Worsted weight yarn as listed in color key
- #16 tapestry needle
- Sawtooth hanger
- Hot-glue gun (optional)

Instructions
1. Cut plastic canvas according to graphs.

2. Stitch plastic canvas following graphs. Back piece will remain unstitched.

3. Using medium taupe through step 4, Whipstitch basket bottom to bottom edges of basket front and back. Whipstitch basket sides to front, back and bottom.

4. Whipstitch front and back handle pieces together above blue dots on graph. Overcast top edges of basket and handles below dots.

5. Glue or stitch sawtooth hanger to center top backside of handle.

—Designed by Joan Green

COLOR KEY	
Worsted Weight Yarn	**Yards**
☐ Light taupe #8765	20
■ Medium taupe #8766	48
■ Light pimento #8827	5
■ Light sea green #8878	3
Uncoded area is natural #8940	
Continental Stitches	14
Color numbers given are for Spinrite Bernat Berella "4" worsted weight yarn.	

HELPFUL HINTS
To keep from losing track of your scissors and needle-threader while stitching, tie each to an end of a long piece of yarn. Wear this crafting "necklace" around your neck every time you work on a project!

Instead of buying containers to hold small craft items such as buttons, beads, bells, etc., use clear 35mm film containers with snap-on lids.

Keep your plastic canvas scraps at your fingertips by storing them in gallon-size resealable plastic bags. Place clear canvas scraps in one bag, white scraps in another and mixed colors in a third bag.

If you craft on a tight budget, be sure to save every last little scrap of yarn in a clear plastic bag. These scraps work just as well as fiberfill for stuffing projects. A penny saved is a penny earned!

INNOVATIVE IDEA
How about this for a smart use of plastic canvas? If your window screen ever gets a small hole in it, patch it with a small piece of 14-count canvas. It's far less expensive than buying a new screen, and will keep the bugs out just as well!

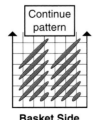

Continue pattern

Basket Side
7 holes x 40 holes
Cut 2
Basket Bottom
7 holes x 80 holes
Cut 1

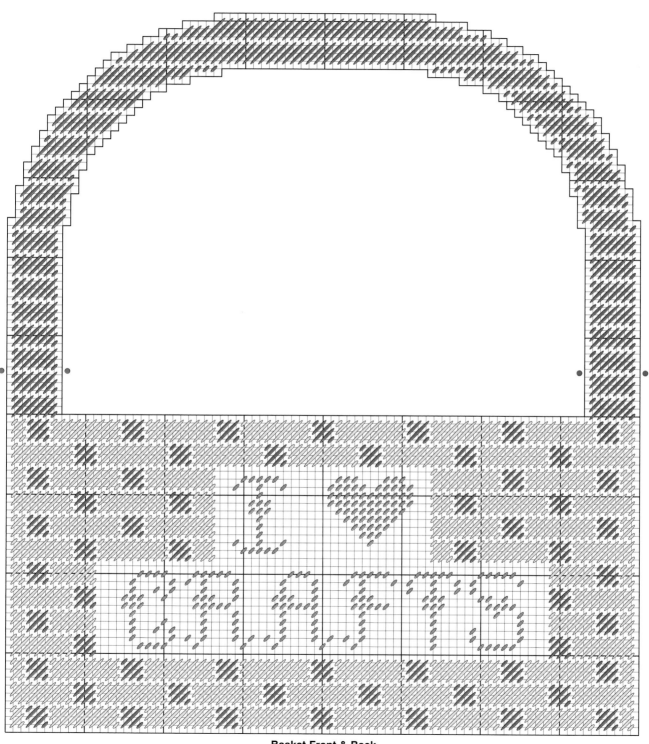

Basket Front & Back
80 holes x 91 holes
Cut 2, stitch 1

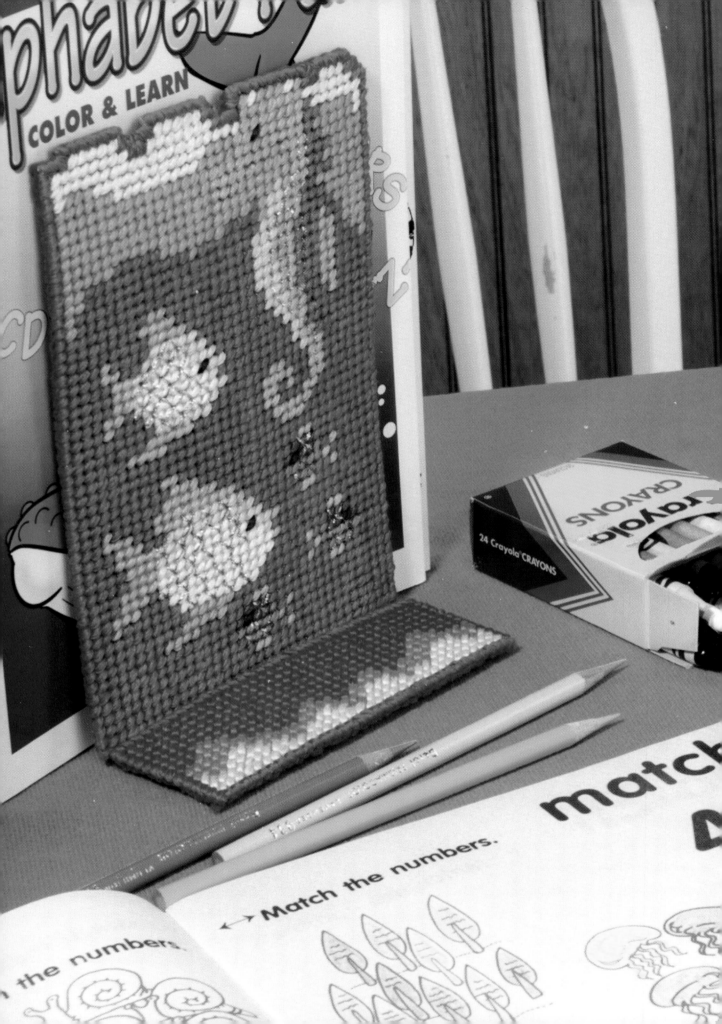

Chapter Four

JUST FOR KIDS!

Include your children in your favorite needlecraft hobby by stitching kids' bedroom decorations that are as fun and colorful as they are practical. Playful door hangers, bright desk sets, a musical bank and other terrific projects will be a delight for you to stitch and winners with your kids!

TROPICAL TREASURES

*Brightly colored creatures of the sea decorate this child's
study set including bookends, pencil can and treasure chest.*

Skill Level: Intermediate

Project Note
Use 18 strands when working with embroidery
floss.

BOOKEND COVERS

Materials
- 1 sheet 7-count plastic canvas
- 6-strand embroidery floss as listed in color key
- 8-ply metallic thread as listed in color key
- 2 (11") squares blue felt
- Sewing needle
- Hot-glue gun

Instructions
1. Cut plastic canvas according to graphs (page 90).

2. Continental Stitch pieces following graphs.
Backstitch with metallic thread over completed
background stitching. Overcast both pieces with
imperial blue.

3. Using top and foot pieces as templates, cut felt to
fit. With sewing needle and 1 strand imperial blue
floss, sew felt to backside of corresponding pieces,
leaving bottom edges of top pieces and top edges of
foot pieces open.

4. Slide completed pieces over bookends; glue foot
pieces to bookends.

PENCIL HOLDER

Materials
- ½ sheet 7-count plastic canvas
- 3" radial plastic canvas circle
- 6-strand embroidery floss as listed in color key
- 8-ply metallic thread as listed in color key
- Light blue felt
- White craft gun

Instructions
1. Cut plastic canvas according to graph (page 91).
From felt, cut one circle slightly smaller than 3"
plastic canvas circle; cut one 4¼" x 8¾" piece.

2. Continental Stitch holder following graph,
overlapping two holes before stitching. Backstitch
with metallic thread over completed background
stitching.

3. With imperial blue, Straight Stitch plastic canvas circle from outermost row of holes to center
holes; work one Cross Stitch in center.

4. Overcast top edge of holder with imperial blue.
Glue felt circle to wrong side of stitched circle.
Glue felt to backside of holder, trimming edges as
necessary.

5. With felt on the inside, Whipstitch circle to
holder with imperial blue.

PIRATE'S CHEST

Materials
- 1 sheet 7-count plastic canvas
- 6-strand embroidery floss as listed in color key
- Yellow-gold felt
- White craft gun

Instructions
1. Cut plastic canvas according to graphs (page 89).

2. From felt, cut two pieces slightly smaller than
sides, one piece slightly smaller than front, one
piece slightly smaller than back, one piece slightly
smaller than lid and one piece slightly smaller than
bottom.

3. Continental Stitch pieces following graphs. Work
French Knot on front, wrapping floss around needle three times.

4. Using dark wheat straw through step 5, Overcast

TROPICAL TREASURES

top edges of front and sides; Overcast front and side edges of lid.

5. Whipstitch chest front, back and sides together. With wrong side of bottom on the inside, Whipstitch bottom to front, back and sides. Whipstitch back edge of lid to top edge of back.

6. For loop, cut a 2½"–3" length of dark coffee

brown. Thread ends from front to back where indicated on graph. Make loop long enough to twist once and loop around French Knot; knot or glue ends to backside.

7. Apply a thin line of glue around edges of felt pieces and attach to inside of box.

—Designed by Kathleen Marie O'Donnell

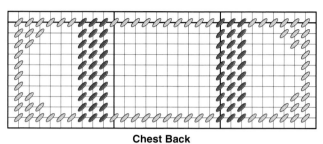

Chest Back
29 holes x 11 holes
Cut 1

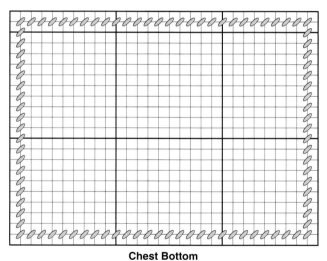

Chest Bottom
29 holes x 22 holes
Cut 1

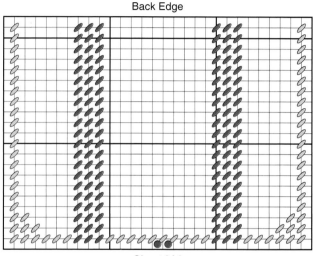

Back Edge

Chest Lid
29 holes x 22 holes
Cut 1

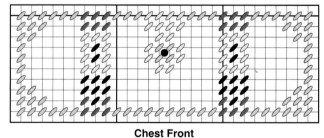

Chest Front
29 holes x 11 holes
Cut 1

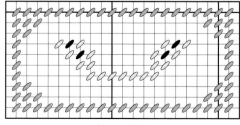

Chest Side
22 holes x 11 holes
Cut 2

COLOR KEY
PIRATE'S CHEST

6-Strand Embroidery Floss	Skeins
■ Russet #434	3
□ Deep topaz #725	1
▨ Dark wheat straw #729	5
■ Dark coffee brown #801	1
Uncoded areas are imperial blue #995 Continental Stitches	9
● Dark coffee brown #801 French Knot	
● Attach loop	

Color numbers given are for DMC 6-strand embroidery floss.

Heart & Home Expressions 89

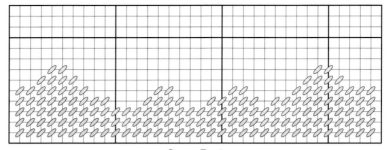

Cover Foot
35 holes x 13 holes
Cut 2

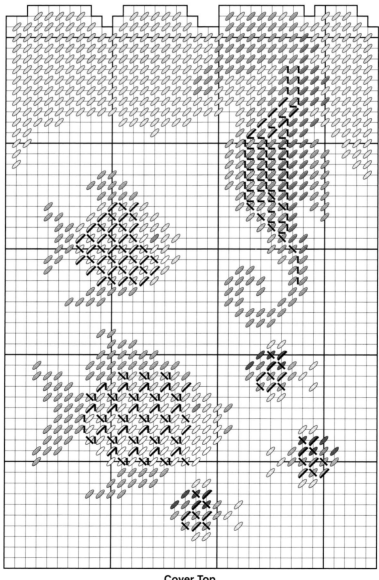

Cover Top
35 holes x 53 holes
Cut 2

COLOR KEY
BOOKEND COVERS

6-Strand Embroidery Floss	Skeins
■ Russet #434	1
☐ Deep canary #444	1
☐ Light lemon #445	1
■ Christmas green #699	1
▨ Kelly green #701	1
☐ Chartreuse #704	1
▨ Deep topaz #725	1
▨ Medium tangerine #741	2
☐ Very light pearl gray #762	3
▨ Gold #783	2
■ Very dark royal blue #820	1
☐ Peacock blue #996	3
☐ Very light golden yellow #3078	1
Uncoded areas are imperial blue #995 Continental Stitches	11
8-Ply Metallic Thread	**Reels**
⁄ Misty sunset #1900 Backstitch	1

Color numbers given are for DMC 6-strand embroidery floss and Kreinik Ombre 8-ply metallic thread.

COLOR KEY
PENCIL HOLDER

6-Strand Embroidery Floss	Skeins
■ Russet #434	1
☐ Deep canary #444	1
☐ Light lemon #445	1
■ Christmas green #699	1
▨ Kelly green #701	1
☐ Chartreuse #704	1
▨ Deep topaz #725	1
▨ Medium tangerine #741	1
☐ Very light pearl gray #762	1
▨ Gold #783	1
■ Very dark royal blue #820	1
☐ Peacock blue #996	1
☐ Very light golden yellow #3078	1
■ Fuchsia #3607	1
▨ Light fuchsia #3608	1
Uncoded areas are imperial blue #995 Continental Stitches	9
8-Ply Metallic Thread	**Reels**
⁄ Misty sunset #1900 Backstitch	1

Color numbers given are for DMC 6-strand embroidery floss and Kreinik Ombre 8-ply metallic thread.

Overlap   Overlap

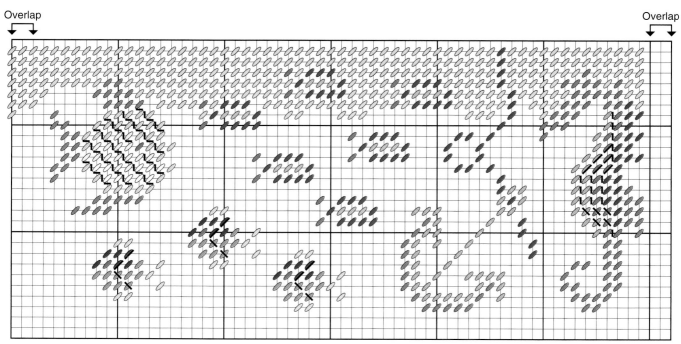

Pencil Holder
62 holes x 28 holes
Cut 1

JUST FOR KIDS!

TEDDY BEAR MUSICAL BANK

Super-soft chenille yarn makes this adorable teddy bear bank soft and cuddly while the musical coin slot makes saving money fun for youngsters!

Skill Level: Advanced beginner

Materials
- 1 sheet 7-count stiff plastic canvas
- Chenille yarn as listed in color key
- Plastic canvas yarn as listed in color key
- #5 pearl cotton as listed in color key
- #16 and #18 tapestry needles
- Music bank #P10693-43
- 12" ⅝"-wide grosgrain ribbon (red with white dots)
- ⅝" round hook-and-loop tape
- Craft glue

Project Note
When stitching with chenille yarn, work with 12" lengths only.

Instructions
1. Cut plastic canvas according to graphs (right and page 94). Cut two 10-hole x 39-hole pieces for bank sides and one 31-hole x 10-hole piece for bank bottom. Teddy bear back and bank bottom, back and door will remain unstitched.

2. Stitch teddy bear front following graph. Work Backstitches over completed background stitching. Stitch bank top and bank sides with brick chenille yarn Continental Stitches. Do not Overcast inside edges of bank top.

3. Using brick chenille yarn through step 5, Whipstitch bank top and sides together, then Whipstitch bank top and sides to teddy bear back where indicated on graph. *Note: Bank bottom will be added later.*

4. Whipstitch bottom edge of door to bank back where indicated on graph. Whipstitch bank back to bank top and sides.

5. Whipstitch teddy bear front to teddy bear back along side and top edges. Whipstitch bank bottom

to bottom edges of teddy bear front and back and bottom edges of bank sides and back.

6. Insert music bank into top opening of bank. *Note: Music will play whenever a coin is inserted.* Glue one piece of hook-and-loop tape to inside of tab on door. Center and glue remaining piece above opening on bank back so pieces will connect.

7. Tie grosgrain ribbon into a bow and glue to bear as desired.

—Designed by Cherie Marie Leck

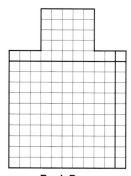

Bank Door
11 holes x 15 holes
Cut 1
Do not stitch

COLOR KEY	
Chenille Yarn	**Yards**
☐ Sandstone #155	7
Uncoded areas are brick #134	
Continental Stitches	55
Plastic Canvas Yarn	
■ Black #00	2
╱ Black #00 Backstitch	
#5 Pearl Cotton	
╱ Black #310 Backstitch	3
╱ Whipstitch to bank top, bottom and sides	
╱ Whipstitch to door	
Color numbers given are for Lion Brand Chenille yarn, Uniek Needloft plastic canvas yarn and DMC #5 pearl cotton.	

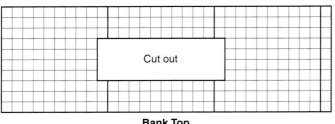

TEDDY BEAR MUSICAL BANK

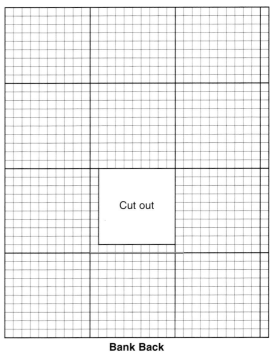

Bank Top
31 holes x 10 holes
Cut and stitch 1

Bank Back
31 holes x 39 holes
Cut 1
Do not stitch

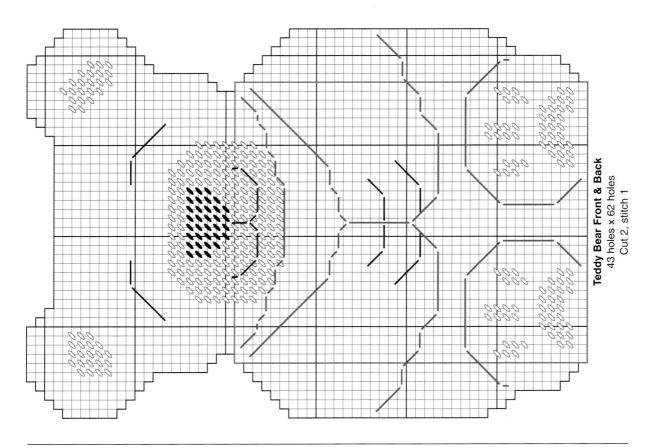

Teddy Bear Front & Back
43 holes x 62 holes
Cut 2, stitch 1

SUMMERTIME SWINGS

Stitch these playful personalized door hangers for your children to remind them that summer is always just around the corner!

Skill Level: Intermediate

Materials

Each Hanger
- ⅓ sheet 7-count plastic canvas
- Worsted weight yarn as listed in color key
- Plastic canvas yarn as listed in color key
- #16 tapestry needle
- Hot-glue gun

Instructions

1. Cut plastic canvas according to graphs (below and page 97).

2. Stitch pieces following graphs. Over completed background stitching, Backstitch heart pattern on girl's jumper with 4 plies yarn and mouths and outlining on boy's romper with 2 plies yarn. Use 2 plies yarn for all French Knots.

3. Using arrow on nameplate as center point, center and Backstitch name with 4 plies yarn where indicated on graph, allowing one bar between letters.

4. Overcast nameplate with red, boy's romper with deep colonial blue and remaining edges with adjacent colors.

5. For hair bow, using 2 plies of a 6" length of daffodil, thread ends from back to front through holes indicated on graph. Tie in a small bow, trimming ends as necessary.

6. Cut two 20" lengths of honey yarn for each swing. Working with one length at a time, make a twisted cord from each by holding one end in one hand and opposite end in other hand. Twist ends in opposite directions until yarn begins to twist.

7. Bring two ends together and hold firmly; run finger between the two strands to the fold, allowing yarn to twist, forming a ropelike strand.

8. Glue folded ends to back of nameplate at blue lines. Trim ends so ropelike strands are exactly the same length and glue to backsides of swings at blue lines. Lightly glue cords to front sides of kids' hands.

—Designed by Joan Green

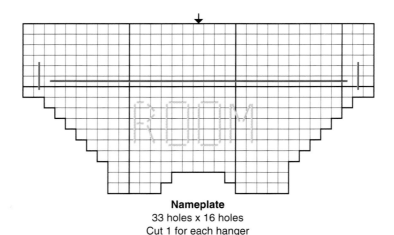

Nameplate
33 holes x 16 holes
Cut 1 for each hanger

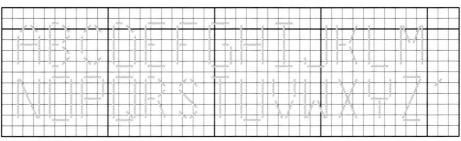

Alphabet

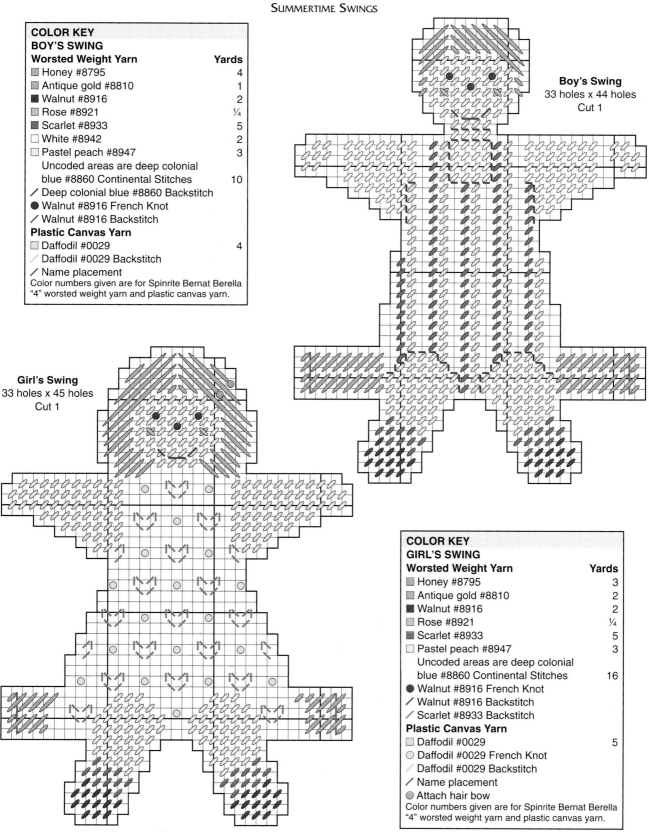

COLOR KEY
BOY'S SWING

Worsted Weight Yarn	Yards
▨ Honey #8795	4
▨ Antique gold #8810	1
▪ Walnut #8916	2
▨ Rose #8921	¼
▪ Scarlet #8933	5
☐ White #8942	2
☐ Pastel peach #8947	3
Uncoded areas are deep colonial blue #8860 Continental Stitches	10
╱ Deep colonial blue #8860 Backstitch	
● Walnut #8916 French Knot	
╱ Walnut #8916 Backstitch	

Plastic Canvas Yarn

☐ Daffodil #0029	4
╱ Daffodil #0029 Backstitch	
╱ Name placement	

Color numbers given are for Spinrite Bernat Berella "4" worsted weight yarn and plastic canvas yarn.

Boy's Swing
33 holes x 44 holes
Cut 1

Girl's Swing
33 holes x 45 holes
Cut 1

COLOR KEY
GIRL'S SWING

Worsted Weight Yarn	Yards
▨ Honey #8795	3
▨ Antique gold #8810	2
▪ Walnut #8916	2
▨ Rose #8921	¼
▪ Scarlet #8933	5
☐ Pastel peach #8947	3
Uncoded areas are deep colonial blue #8860 Continental Stitches	16
● Walnut #8916 French Knot	
╱ Walnut #8916 Backstitch	
╱ Scarlet #8933 Backstitch	

Plastic Canvas Yarn

☐ Daffodil #0029	5
○ Daffodil #0029 French Knot	
╱ Daffodil #0029 Backstitch	
╱ Name placement	
● Attach hair bow	

Color numbers given are for Spinrite Bernat Berella "4" worsted weight yarn and plastic canvas yarn.

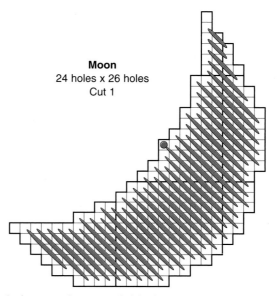

NURSERY RHYME TIME

Stitch this delightful Hey, Diddle Diddle *mobile and* Cow Jumped Over the Moon *switch-plate cover for the nursery.*

Skill Level: Intermediate

Project Note
When working with plastic lacing, cut ends at an angle to make insertion easier. Do not use a needle. Keep lacing smooth and flat. To prevent twisting and tangling, guide lacing between thumb and forefinger of free hand.

HEY, DIDDLE DIDDLE MOBILE

Materials
- 1 sheet 7-count plastic canvas
- Plastic canvas yarn as listed in color key
- Glow-in-the-dark plastic lacing as listed in color key
- 6-strand embroidery floss as listed in color key
- 3 yards ¼"-wide light blue ribbon
- 2½ yards ¼"-wide white ribbon
- 10" craft wire ring
- Sewing needle
- White and light blue sewing thread
- Hot-glue gun or craft glue

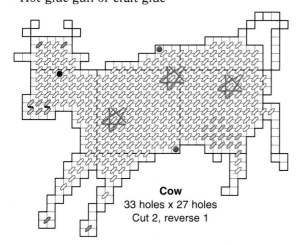

Moon
24 holes x 26 holes
Cut 1

Cow
33 holes x 27 holes
Cut 2, reverse 1

Cow & Moon
1. Cut plastic canvas according to graphs.

2. Stitch cows following graph, reversing one cow

before stitching. With black yarn, work French Knots and Backstitches on cow over completed Continental Stitches. With white glow-in-the-dark lacing, Straight Stitch stars on cow.

3. Whipstitch wrong sides of cow together at hooves and horns with gray and at remaining edges with adjacent colors.

4. Stitch moon with one 2-yard length of lacing. Overcast edges with eggshell, catching ends of lacing while Overcasting to anchor and conceal them.

Cat
1. Cut plastic canvas according to graph.

2. Continental Stitch cats following graph, reversing one before stitching. With yarn, work French Knots for eyes and Backstitches for mouth. With 3 strands black floss, Backstitch over eyes.

3. Straight Stitch fiddle strings with 6 strands gold floss. Work cinnamon Straight Stitches at bottom and center of fiddle strings.

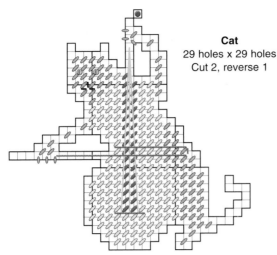

Cat
29 holes x 29 holes
Cut 2, reverse 1

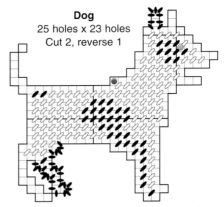

Dog
25 holes x 23 holes
Cut 2, reverse 1

indicated with colors given, nose and tail edges with black, inside of mouth with red, and remaining edges with adjacent colors.

Dish & Spoon
27 holes x 27 holes
Cut 2, reverse 1

4. With wrong sides together, Whipstitch edges indicated with colors given, tail edges with gray, bow and neck of fiddle with cinnamon, and remaining edges with adjacent colors.

COLOR KEY	
Plastic Canvas Yarn	**Yards**
■ Black #00	5⅓
☐ Sundown #10	5
■ Cinnamon #14	2
☐ Gold #17	2
■ Cerulean #34	2
■ Gray #38	7½
☐ Beige #40	3
☐ White #41	37
■ Dark royal #48	7
☐ Fleshtone #56	3
Red #02 Whipstitching	½
Eggshell #39 Whipstitching	2
╱ Cinnamon #14 Straight Stitch	
● Black #00 French Knot	
╱ Black #00 Straight Stitch	
● Cerulean #34 French Knot	
Plastic Lacing	
▨ White glow-in-the-dark	5
╱ White glow-in-the-dark Backstitch	
6-Strand Embroidery Floss	
╱ Black #310 Backstitch	⅓
╱ Gold #783 Straight Stitch	1
● Attach ribbon	
Color numbers given are for Uniek Needloft plastic canvas yarn and DMC 6-strand embroidery floss.	

Dog

1. Cut plastic canvas according to graph.

2. Continental Stitch dogs following graph, reversing one before stitching. Work cerulean French Knots for eyes.

3. With wrong sides together, Whipstitch edges

Dish & Spoon

1. Cut plastic canvas according to graph.

2. Continental Stitch pieces following graph, reversing one before stitching. With 2 plies black yarn, work French Knots and Backstitches over completed background stitching.

3. With wrong sides together, Whipstitch dish edges together with cerulean, arm and leg areas of spoon with gold and remaining edges with beige.

Assembly

1. To attach ribbon through step 4, thread end through hole in plastic canvas or loop around craft ring. Bring end up ½"; Whipstitch ribbon together with sewing needle and matching thread.

2. At holes indicated on graphs, attach a 4½"

Fig. 1

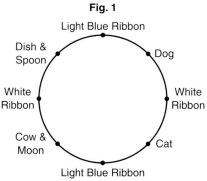

length of light blue ribbon to top hole on cow and one end of a 4¼" length of light blue ribbon to bottom hole on cow and remaining end to moon. Attach a 7" length of white ribbon to cat, an 11½" length of light blue ribbon to dog and a 7½" length of white ribbon to dish.

3. Following Fig. 1 throughout, attach free ends of ribbons to craft ring. Cut one 18" length each from light blue and white ribbon. Attach ends to craft ring.

4. Cut light blue ribbon at desired length for hanging (sample used a 19" length). Tie a loop in one end. Attach remaining end to center of 18" lengths of blue and white ribbon.

5. Hold remaining lengths of white and light blue ribbon side by side. Glue ends to craft ring. Wrap ribbons around ring, adjusting for attached hanging ribbons. Glue ends to ring, cutting off excess ribbon.

6. Hang mobile by top loop as desired.

COW JUMPED OVER THE MOON SWITCH-PLATE COVER

Materials
- ¼ sheet 7-count plastic canvas
- Plastic canvas yarn as listed in color key
- Glow-in-the-dark plastic lacing as listed in color key
- Double-stick foam tape

Instructions

1. Cut plastic canvas according to graph.

2. Stitch piece following graph. With black yarn, work French Knot and Backstitches on cow over completed Continental Stitches. With white glow-

in-the-dark lacing, Straight Stitch stars on cow.

3. Overcast edges indicated with colors given, hooves and horns with gray, tail and legs with white and remaining inside and outer edges with adjacent colors (see photo).

4. Attach cover to switch plate with double-stick foam tape.

—Designed by Kathleen Kennebeck

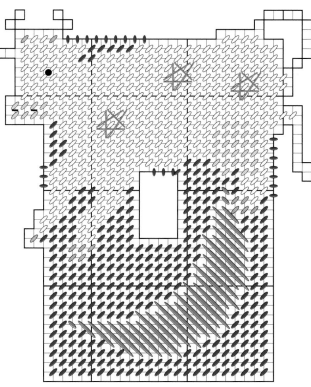

Switch-Plate Cover
33 holes x 39 holes
Cut 1

BALLOON BEAR SET

Stitch this tissue box cover and trinket box combo featuring a whimsical teddy bear for fun yet practical kids' room decorations.

Skill Level: Beginner

Materials
- 3 sheets 7-count plastic canvas
- Plastic canvas yarn as listed in color key
- 6-strand embroidery floss as listed in color key
- 1 yard ¼"-wide light blue satin ribbon
- 6 (½") light brown pompons
- 6 (¼") black pompons
- 8 (¼") pink pompons
- 8 (11mm) movable eyes
- Craft glue

TISSUE BOX COVER

1. Cut plastic canvas according to graphs (page 104).

2. Stitch pieces following graphs, stitching one side with a holly green balloon, one with a Christmas red balloon, one with a royal blue balloon and one with an orange balloon. Backstitch with gray floss over completed background stitching.

3. Using photo as a guide, on each side, glue one light brown pompon to lower front of bear's head. Glue one black pompon to the left and one pink pompon to the right of light brown pompon. Glue one movable eye above pink pompon.

3. Using yellow throughout, Overcast bottom edges

of sides and inside edges of top. Whipstitch sides together, then Whipstitch top to sides.

TRINKET BOX

1. Cut plastic canvas according to graph below. Cut two 29-hole by 29-hole pieces for box short sides and one 29-hole x 57-hole piece for box bottom. Box bottom will remain unstitched.

2. Stitch large sides following graph. Backstitch with gray floss and Straight Stitch with light blue satin ribbon over completed background stitching. With yellow, Continental Stitch box short sides.

3. For bows, thread a 12" length of satin ribbon from back to front at holes indicated on each large side. Tie ribbon in a bow and trim ends as desired.

4. Using photo as guide, for each face, glue one light brown pompon to center of head. Glue movable eyes above and pink pompon on each side of the light brown pompon. Glue one black pompon to center front of light brown pompon.

5. Using yellow throughout, Overcast top edges of sides. Whipstitch sides together, then Whipstitch bottom to sides.

—Designed by Nancy Marshall

Trinket Box Large Side
57 holes x 29 holes
Cut 2

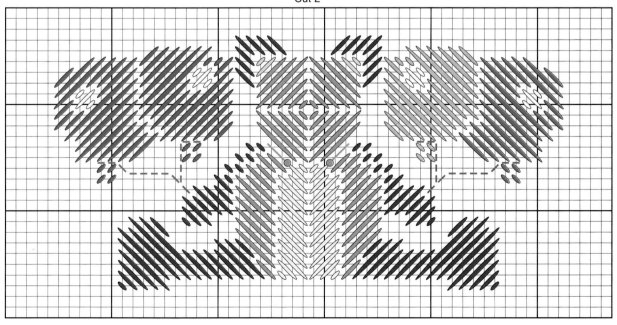

COLOR KEY

Plastic Canvas Yarn	Yards
☐ White #01	2
■ Royal blue #09	6
☐ Powder pink #11	1
■ Burnt orange #17	5
■ Christmas red #19	5
■ Holly green #31	6
■ Camel #34	12
■ Bark #44	19
☐ Sandstone #47	3
Uncoded areas are yellow #26	
Continental Stitches	95

6-Strand Embroidery Floss

╱ Light steel gray #318 Backstitch	2

¼"-Wide Satin Ribbon

╱ Light blue Straight Stitch

● Attach bow

Color numbers given are for Darice Nylon Plus plastic canvas yarn and DMC 6-strand embroidery floss.

Tissue Box Cover Side
30 holes x 36 holes
Cut 4
Stitch 1 balloon with Christmas red
1 with royal blue
1 with holly green
1 with burnt orange

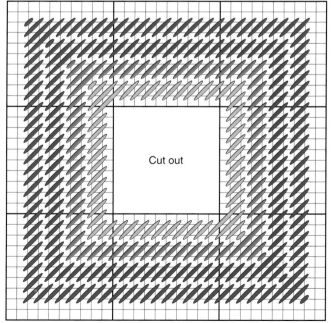

Tissue Box Cover Top
30 holes x 30 holes
Cut 1

Cut out

CRAYON PHOTO FRAME

Your young boy or girl will love displaying his or her class picture in this delightful photo frame! Be sure to stitch the crayon in your child's favorite color.

Skill Level: Advanced beginner

Materials
- ½ sheet 7-count stiff plastic canvas
- ¼ sheet 7-count soft plastic canvas
- Plastic canvas yarn as listed in color key
- Small amount black 6-strand embroidery floss
- #16 or #18 tapestry needle
- 3" x 7⅞" piece cardboard
- Glue or tape

Instructions

1. Cut crayon from soft plastic canvas and frame front and back from stiff plastic canvas according to graphs (below and page 107). Cut photo opening on front only. Cut two 17-hole x 31-hole pieces for frame stand from stiff plastic canvas.

2. Stitch frame front and crayon following graphs, working embroidery over completed background stitching. Frame back and stand pieces will remain unstitched.

3. Using white throughout, Whipstitch stand pieces together along side and bottom edges. Center stand on frame back, making sure bottom edges are even.

Whipstitch top edges of stand to frame back.

4. Cut a 4½" length of white yarn. Approximately 1" from bottom, thread one end through center of stand. Make ends equal in length; tie a knot next to stand. Thread one end through center of frame back 1" from bottom; tie ends in a knot.

5. With yellow, Overcast bottom edge of front between dots; Overcast top, left and bottom sides of photo opening. With burgundy, Overcast point and bottom edge of crayon.

6. With adjacent colors, Whipstitch left side of crayon to bar on frame front where indicated on graph.

7. Using yellow throughout, Whipstitch frame front to frame back along bottom edges, leaving edges open between dots. Continue Whipstitching edges together to end of striped border above crayon.

8. Whipstitch right side of crayon to right edges of frame front and back with adjacent colors. ***Note:*** *Crayon will be curved.*

9. Center wallet-size photo on cardboard; tape or glue in place. Insert cardboard through bottom opening.

—Designed by Kathy Wirth

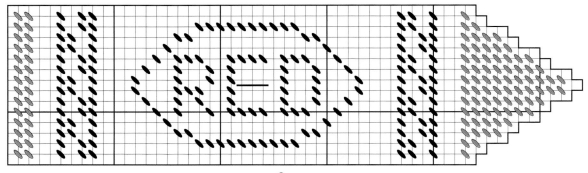

Crayon
15 holes x 54 holes
Cut 1 from soft

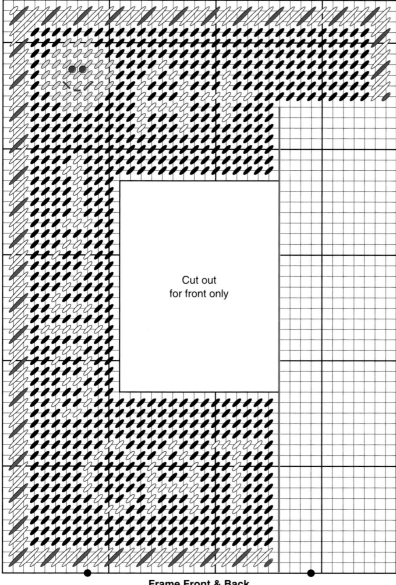

Cut out
for front only

Frame Front & Back
37 holes x 54 holes
Cut 2, stitch 1, from stiff

COLOR KEY

Plastic Canvas Yarn	Yards
■ Black #00	16
■ Christmas red #02	11
▨ Burgundy #03	4
□ White #41	7
▢ Yellow #57	5

Uncoded areas on crayon are
Christmas red #02 Continental
Stitches
/ Black #00 Straight Stitch

6-Strand Embroidery Floss
/ Black Backstitch
● Black French Knot
/ Whipstitch to crayon

Color numbers given are for Uniek Needloft
plastic canvas yarn.

Chapter Five

BATHROOM ACCENTS

*Give your bathroom a pretty
touch with a handy soap
holder and basket, a graceful
swan picture adds beauty to a
wall, and other lovely projects
give a decorator's touch to
your bathroom.*

Roses, Roses

This charming organizer set holds makeup, jewelry,
hairbrushes and hair accessories. With its delicate rosebud pattern and
pretty colors, the set will also be an eye-catching bathroom decoration.

Experience Level: Advanced beginner

Materials
- 1 sheet 7-count stiff plastic canvas
- 2 sheets 7-count regular plastic canvas
- Plastic canvas yarn as listed in color key
- #16 tapestry needle
- Hot-glue gun

Brush & Comb Caddy

1. From regular plastic canvas, cut pieces according to graphs (pages 112 and 113); cut two 1-hole x 35-hole pieces for pocket side spacers, one 1-hole x 14-hole piece for pocket bottom spacer and one 3-hole x 29-hole piece for brush loop. Spacers will remain unstitched.

2. Stitch pieces following graphs. Using eggshell through step 3, Continental Stitch brush loop. Overcast long edges of loop; Whipstitch short edges together. Backstitch seam area of loop to unworked section of pocket.

3. Overcast top edge of pocket and inner and outer edges of caddy. Whipstitch side spacers to pocket sides and bottom spacer to pocket bottom. Whipstitch spacers together. Whipstitch spacers to caddy where indicated on graph.

Vanity Tray

1. Cut tray sides from regular plastic canvas and tray bottom from stiff plastic canvas according to graphs (pages 111–113).

2. Stitch pieces following graphs.

3. Using eggshell through step 4, with wrong sides together, Whipstitch top edges of two short sides together and top edges of two long sides together. Repeat for remaining side pieces.

4. Whipstitch sides together. With right side of bottom facing up, Whipstitch bottom to sides.

Cotton Swab & Cotton Ball Boxes

1. Cut pieces from regular plastic canvas according to graphs (pages 110 and 112).

2. Stitch pieces following graphs.

3. Using eggshell through step 4, Overcast lid top and lid bottom pieces. Overcast top edges of sides. For each box, Whipstitch four sides together; with wrong side of box bottom facing up, Whipstitch bottom to sides.

4. With wrong sides together, center and glue lid bottoms to lid tops.

Decorative Soap Dish

1. Cut pieces from regular plastic canvas according to graphs (page 112).

2. Stitch pieces following graphs.

3. Using eggshell throughout, Overcast top edges of sides. Whipstitch sides together. With wrong side of dish bottom facing up, Whipstitch bottom to sides.

—Designed by Angie Arickx

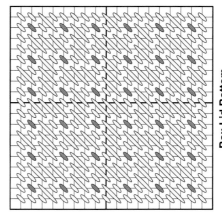

Box Lid Bottom
19 holes x 19 holes
Cut 2 from regular

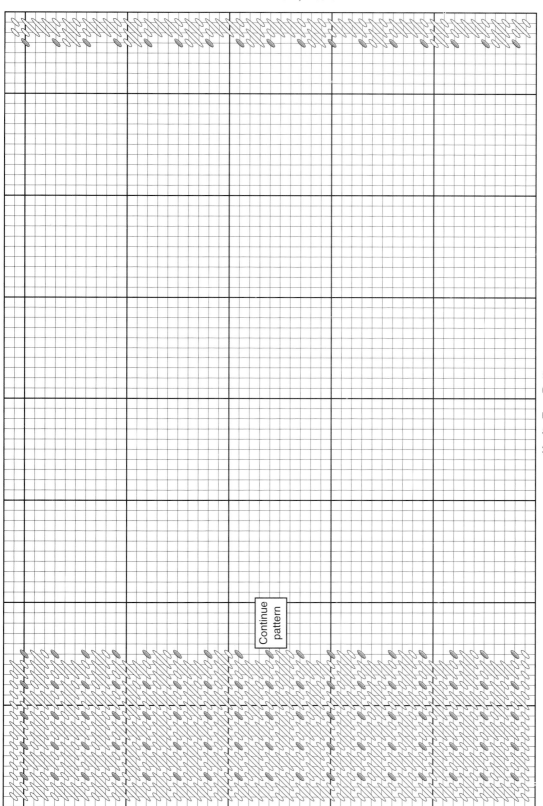

Continue pattern

Vanity Tray Bottom
78 holes x 52 holes
Cut 1 from stiff

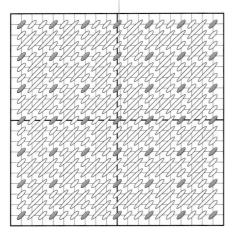

Soap Dish Bottom & Box Bottom
20 holes x 20 holes
Cut 1 from regular for soap dish bottom
Cut 2 from regular for box bottoms

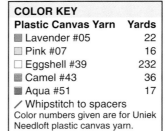

COLOR KEY	
Plastic Canvas Yarn	**Yards**
◼ Lavender #05	22
◻ Pink #07	16
◻ Eggshell #39	232
◻ Camel #43	36
◼ Aqua #51	17
╱ Whipstitch to spacers	
Color numbers given are for Uniek Needloft plastic canvas yarn.	

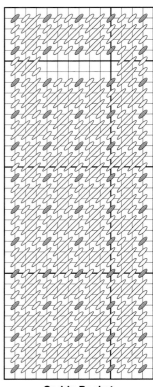

Caddy Pocket
14 holes x 35 holes
Cut 1 from regular

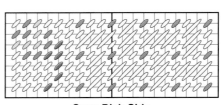

Soap Dish Side
20 holes x 8 holes
Cut 4 from regular

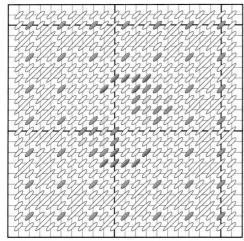

Box Lid Top
22 holes x 22 holes
Cut 2 from regular

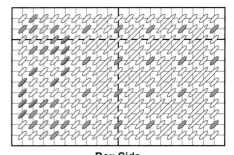

Box Side
20 holes x 13 holes
Cut 8 from regular

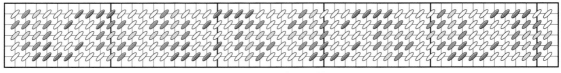

Vanity Tray Short Side
52 holes x 6 holes
Cut 4 from regular

ROSES, ROSES

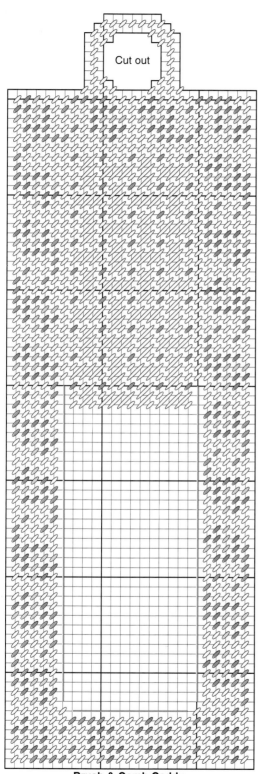

Cut out

Brush & Comb Caddy
26 holes x 79 holes
Cut 1 from regular

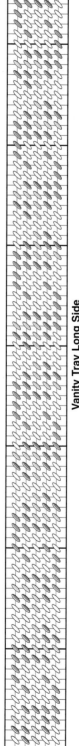

Vanity Tray Long Side
78 holes x 6 holes
Cut 4 from regular

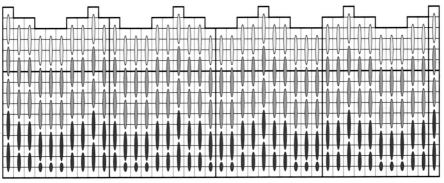

Caddy Long Side
41 holes x 16 holes
Cut 2

BATHROOM ACCENTS

SPARKLING SEASHELLS

Pretty shades of turquoise and peach, accented with peach metallic yarn, give this seashell caddy and potpourri holder set a look that will appeal to both men and women.

Experience Level: Beginner

Materials
- 1⅓ sheets 7-count plastic canvas
- Worsted weight yarn as listed in color key
- ⅛"-wide plastic canvas metallic yarn
- #16 tapestry needle
- White felt (optional)
- Hot-glue gun (optional)

Instructions

1. Cut plastic canvas according to graphs. Cut one 41-hole x 28-hole piece for caddy base and one 28-hole x 28-hole piece for potpourri holder base.

2. Stitch pieces following graphs. Base pieces will remain unstitched.

3. If lining is desired, cut felt slightly smaller than each piece, cutting two pieces for each base. Set aside.

4. With pale ocean, Overcast top edges of caddy long sides. Overcast top edges of caddy short sides and potpourri sides with peach metallic yarn.

5. Whipstitch potpourri sides together from blue dot to blue dot with peach metallic yarn, and remainder of sides together with adjacent colors. Whipstitch bottom to sides with medium ocean.

6. For caddy, Whipstitch short sides to long sides with peach metallic yarn from blue dot to blue dot; Whipstitch remaining side edges together with adjacent colors. Whipstitch sides to bottom with medium ocean.

7. Optional: Glue corresponding lining to top and bottom of base pieces. Glue remaining pieces of lining inside boxes.

—*Designed by Joan Green*

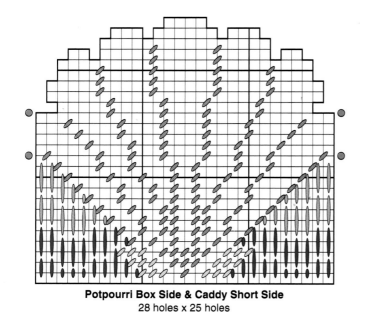

Potpourri Box Side & Caddy Short Side
28 holes x 25 holes
Cut 4 for potpourri box
Cut 2 for caddy

COLOR KEY	
Worsted Weight Yarn	**Yards**
☐ Pale ocean #8760	5
▨ Light ocean #8761	13
■ Medium ocean #8762	17
☐ Medium peach #8978	3
Uncoded areas are light peach #8977 Continental Stitches	34
⅛" Plastic Canvas Metallic Yarn	
▨ Peach #PC 22	
Color numbers given are for Spinrite Bernat Berella "4" worsted weight yarn and Rainbow Gallery Plastic Canvas 7 Metallic Yarn.	

TISSUE KEEPERS

Tuck a box of facial tissues alongside a spare roll of
toilet tissue inside this pretty tissue topper set.

Experience Level: Beginner

Materials

- 2½ sheets 7-count plastic canvas
- Plastic canvas yarn as listed in color key
- #16 tapestry needle

Instructions

1. Cut plastic canvas according to graphs (below and page 118).

2. Continental Stitch pieces following graphs.

3. Using cerulean throughout, Overcast bottom edges of sides and inner edges of tissue box cover top. For each cover, Whipstitch four sides together; Whipstitch tops to sides.

—Designed by Angie Arickx

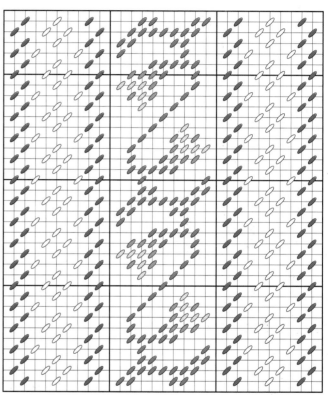

Tissue Box Cover Side &
Spare Roll Cover Side
30 holes x 36 holes
Cut 4 each

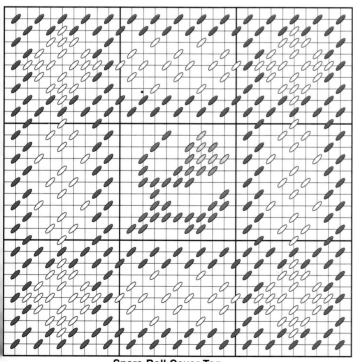

Spare Roll Cover Top
30 holes by 30 holes
Cut 1

COLOR KEY

Plastic Canvas Yarn	Yards
■ Lavender #05	5
□ Pink #07	4
■ Forest #29	17
■ Navy #31	39
□ White #41	31
Uncoded areas are cerulean	
#34 Continental Stitches	150

Color numbers given are for Uniek Needloft plastic canvas yarn.

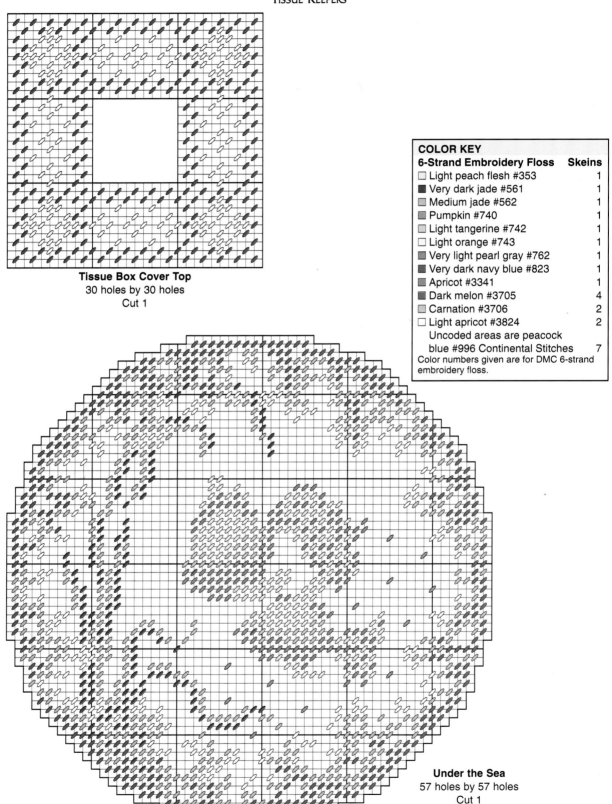

Tissue Box Cover Top
30 holes by 30 holes
Cut 1

COLOR KEY

6-Strand Embroidery Floss	Skeins
□ Light peach flesh #353	1
■ Very dark jade #561	1
▨ Medium jade #562	1
▨ Pumpkin #740	1
□ Light tangerine #742	1
□ Light orange #743	1
▨ Very light pearl gray #762	1
■ Very dark navy blue #823	1
▨ Apricot #3341	1
■ Dark melon #3705	4
▨ Carnation #3706	2
□ Light apricot #3824	2

Uncoded areas are peacock
blue #996 Continental Stitches   7
Color numbers given are for DMC 6-strand
embroidery floss.

Under the Sea
57 holes by 57 holes
Cut 1

UNDER THE SEA

*For those with a bright, tropical theme in their bathroom,
this vibrant picture will be the perfect finishing touch!*

Experience Level
Advanced beginner

Materials
- 1 sheet 7-count plastic canvas
- 6-strand embroidery floss as listed in color key
- 9" square piece coordinating felt
- White glue

Instructions
1. Cut plastic canvas according to graph (page 118). Using plastic canvas piece as a template, cut felt slightly smaller than piece.

2. Continental Stitch piece with 18 strands floss following graph. Overcast piece with 18 strands dark coral.

3. With 12 strands dark coral, make a loop of desired length and attach with a double knot to center top backside of stitched piece.

4. Apply glue to felt and attach to backside of stitched piece.

—Designed by Kathleen Marie O'Donnell

GRACEFUL SWAN

This lovely scene pictures elegant swans surrounded by an array of flowers. Stitch this piece to hang on a wall or door.

Experience Level: Advanced beginner

Materials
- ½ sheet 7-count plastic canvas
- 6-strand embroidery floss as listed in color key
- 5 (½") pink buttons
- 6½" square blue felt
- White glue

Instructions

1. Cut plastic canvas according to graph.

2. Continental Stitch piece with 18 strands floss following graph. When background stitching is completed, with 6 strands dark antique blue, outline top edges of swans and work French Knots for eyes.

3. With 18 strands floss, work light jade Backstitches and pale yellow, light melon and very light antique blue French Knots. With light melon floss, sew on buttons where indicated on graph.

4. Overcast around side and bottom edges from dot to dot with Wedgwood blue and remaining edges with dark antique blue.

5. Cut a 2" length of dark antique blue floss. Thread ends of floss from front to back at center of top edge. Knot ends on backside. Using finished piece as a template, cut felt to fit; glue to backside.

—Designed by Kathleen Marie O'Donnell

Graceful Swan
41 holes x 44 holes
Cut 1

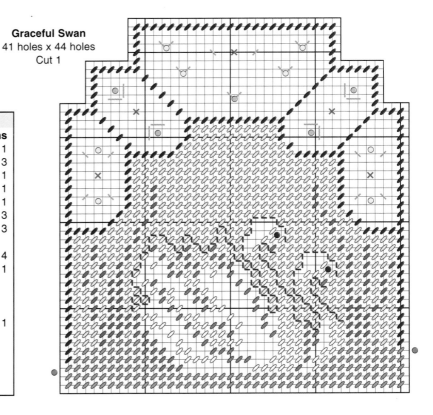

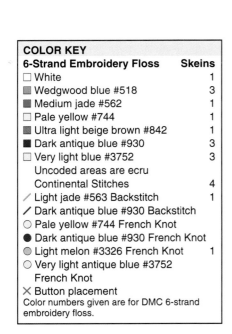

COLOR KEY

6-Strand Embroidery Floss	Skeins
☐ White	1
▨ Wedgwood blue #518	3
▨ Medium jade #562	1
☐ Pale yellow #744	1
▨ Ultra light beige brown #842	1
■ Dark antique blue #930	3
☐ Very light blue #3752	3
Uncoded areas are ecru Continental Stitches	4
╱ Light jade #563 Backstitch	1
╱ Dark antique blue #930 Backstitch	
◯ Pale yellow #744 French Knot	
● Dark antique blue #930 French Knot	
◉ Light melon #3326 French Knot	1
◯ Very light antique blue #3752 French Knot	
✕ Button placement	

Color numbers given are for DMC 6-strand embroidery floss.

DO NOT DISTURB

*Make sure all visitors to the bathroom can enjoy
an uninterrupted stay with this tasteful,
yet to-the-point, door hanger.*

Experience Level: Advanced beginner

Materials
- 1 sheet 10-count plastic canvas
- #3 pearl cotton as listed in color key
- 12" ivory braid or cord
- 18" ⅛"-wide dark blue satin ribbon
- 28" ½"-wide ivory lace trim
- 6" x 3½" piece ivory felt
- White glue

Instructions

1. Cut plastic canvas according to graphs (page 124).

2. Continental Stitch lettering and flowers on borders following graphs. Fill in background on floral border and behind letters in center of sign with ecru Continental Stitches. Do not work Running Stitch around edges at this time.

3. For background stitching inside floral border and around lettering in sign center, stitch long diagonal Straight Stitches with baby pink from border to border or from border to completed stitching in center. Couch diagonal stitches with ecru Continental Stitches following graphs.

4. Cut dark blue satin ribbon in half and thread one length from back to front on each sign through holes indicated on graphs. Tie each in a bow and secure with glue. Trim ends as desired.

5. For hanger, attach ends of cord to "Busy" sign where indicated on graph by running cord through a few stitches on back of sign. Secure with glue.

6. Glue felt to backside of one sign. With wrong sides together, place lace trim between the two signs around edges (see photo). Stitch signs together with an ecru Running Stitch, catching bottom edge of lace trim with each stitch and easing in fullness around corners.

—Designed by Kathleen Marie O'Donnell

COLOR KEY

#3 Pearl Cotton	Skeins
☐ Ecru	3
■ Medium lavender #208	1
☐ Light lavender #211	1
☐ Light cranberry #604	1
■ Bright Christmas green #700	1
☐ Dark parrot green #702	1
☐ Deep canary #725	1
☐ Very light topaz #727	1
☐ Baby pink #818	1
■ Medium blue #826	1
☐ Very light blue #827	1
■ Light terra cotta #920	1
╱ Baby pink #818 Straight Stitch	
● Attach cord	
● Attach dark blue satin ribbon	

Color numbers given are for DMC #3 pearl cotton.

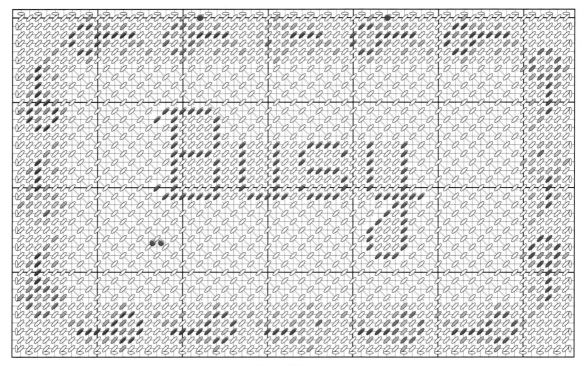

Busy Sign
66 holes x 41 holes
Cut 1

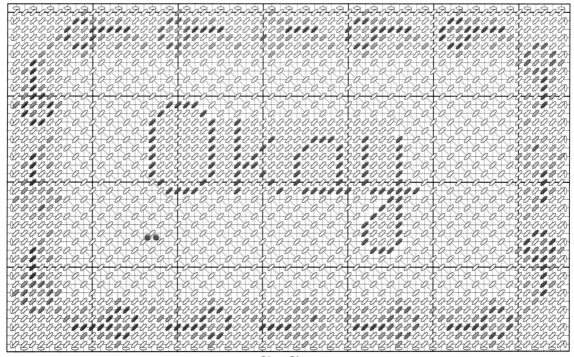

Okay Sign
66 holes x 41 holes
Cut 1

ROSEBUDS & LACE

*Stitch this sweet tissue box cover and potpourri
container in colors to match your bathroom.
It's as pretty as it is practical!*

Experience Level: Intermediate

Materials
- 2½ sheets 7-count plastic canvas
- Worsted weight yarn as listed in color key
- Plastic canvas metallic yarn as listed in color key
- #16 tapestry needle
- 6" white/white roses per yard
- 2½" square coordinating felt (optional)
- Hot-glue gun

Instructions
1. Cut plastic canvas according to graphs (page 127). Cut one 21-hole x 21-hole piece for potpourri holder base. Holder base will remain unstitched. If lining is desired, cut felt to fit holder base.

2. Following graphs, stitch rosebuds on cover sides and holder sides with slanting stitches; Continental Stitch backgrounds with pale sea green. Stitch cover top with Slanting Gobelin Stitches following graph.

3. With 2 plies white, work French Knots and Straight Stitches over completed background stitching. For centers of rosebuds, work gold French Knots in diagonal rows.

4. Overcast inside edges of tissue box cover top with white. Using pale sea green through step 4, Overcast bottom edges of tissue box cover sides and top edges of potpourri holder.

5. Whipstitch cover sides together, then Whipstitch sides to cover top. Whipstitch holder sides together, then Whipstitch sides to holder base.

6. Carefully cut ribbon rosebuds with bow from roses per yard. Glue one to each corner at top of tissue box cover and top of potpourri holder. If desired, glue felt to holder base.

—Designed by Joan Green

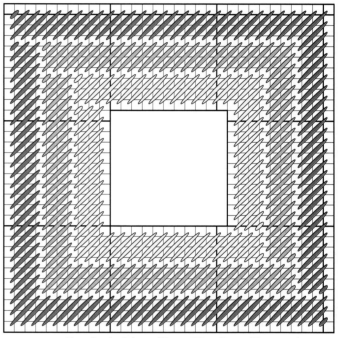

Rosebuds & Lace Tissue Box Cover Top
31 holes x 31 holes
Cut 1

Rosebuds & Lace Potpourri Holder Side
21 holes x 21 holes
Cut 4

COLOR KEY

Worsted Weight Yarn	Yards
☐ Baby yellow #8945	12
☐ Light peach #8977	13
☐ Rose #8921	15
Uncoded areas are pale sea green #8879 Continental Stitches	100
○ White #8942 French Knot	24
╱ White #8942 Straight Stitch	
¹⁄₁₆ " **Plastic Canvas Metallic Yarn**	
● Gold #PM 51 French Knot	10

Color numbers given are for Spinrite Bernat Berella "4" worsted weight yarn and Rainbow Gallery Plastic Canvas 10 Metallic Yarn.

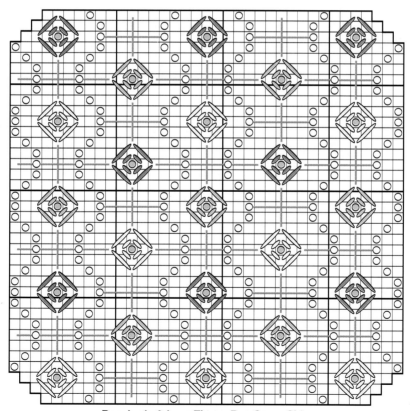

Rosebuds & Lace Tissue Box Cover Side
37 holes x 37 holes
Cut 4

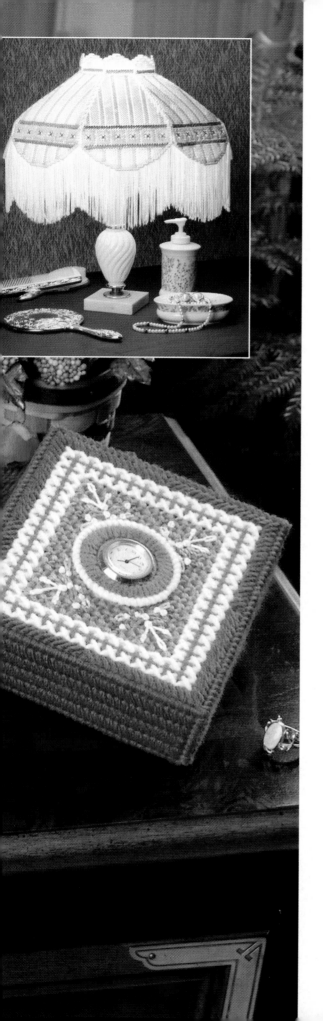

Chapter Six

BEDROOM COMFORTS

Make your bedroom a haven in which you find relaxation and comfort for your body and mind by stitching beautiful items for this special room. An elegant vanity tray, pretty jewelry keepers, a Victorian lamp shade, and many more exquisite designs will be a pleasure to stitch and use!

CLASSIC VANITY SET

A large makeup tray and matching jewelry box
with timepiece will add a pretty touch to the
top of your bureau or vanity.

Experience Level: Advanced beginner

Materials
- 3 sheets 7-count stiff plastic canvas
- 3" plastic canvas radial circle
- Worsted weight yarn as listed in color key
- #3 pearl cotton as listed in color key
- 8 (1⅝") squares craft foam in coordinating color
- White Arabic assembled movement clock face #31-4040
- Hot-glue gun

Instructions

1. Cut plastic canvas according to graphs (pages 131 and 132). Cut the three outermost rows of holes from the radial circle, then cut the three innermost circular threads, leaving the spokes when cutting the third innermost circular thread. ***Note:*** *Spokes will hold yarn and clock in place.*

2. Stitch plastic canvas with yarn following graphs. Work embroidery with pearl cotton over completed background stitching.

3. With raspberry yarn, Straight Stitch circle from the outermost row of holes to the innermost row of spaces created by the spokes, using two stitches per space as necessary. Overcast outer edge of circle with white.

4. Using periwinkle throughout, Overcast bottom edges of lid sides and top edges of box and tray sides. Whipstitch sides of tray together, sides of box together and sides of lid together. Whipstitch tray bottom to tray sides, box bottom to box sides and lid top to lid sides.

5. Insert clock in cutout center of radial circle. Center and glue circle to box lid. ***Note:*** *The hole allows clock to be removed to change battery and reset the time.* Glue craft foam to inside corners of tray sides.

—*Designed by Celia Lange Designs*

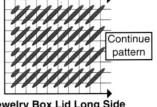

Jewelry Box Lid Long Side
37 holes x 9 holes
Cut 2

Jewelry Box Lid Short Side
33 holes x 9 holes
Cut 2

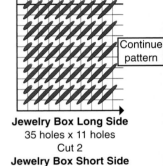

Jewelry Box Long Side
35 holes x 11 holes
Cut 2

Jewelry Box Short Side
31 holes x 11 holes
Cut 2

Jewelry Box Bottom
31 holes x 35 holes
Cut 1

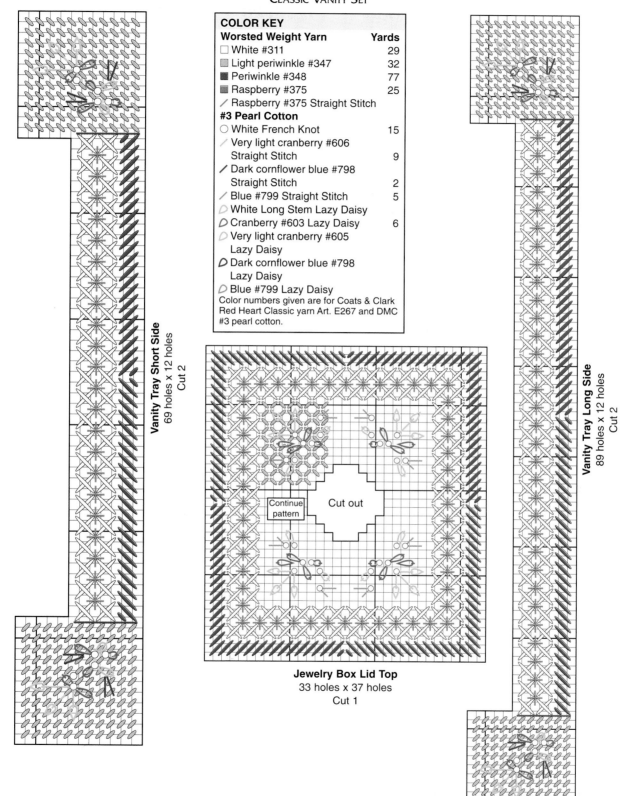

Classic Vanity Set

COLOR KEY

Worsted Weight Yarn	Yards
☐ White #311	29
☐ Light periwinkle #347	32
■ Periwinkle #348	77
■ Raspberry #375	25
╱ Raspberry #375 Straight Stitch	

#3 Pearl Cotton

	Yards
○ White French Knot	15
╱ Very light cranberry #606 Straight Stitch	9
╱ Dark cornflower blue #798 Straight Stitch	2
╱ Blue #799 Straight Stitch	5
⊘ White Long Stem Lazy Daisy	
⊘ Cranberry #603 Lazy Daisy	6
⊘ Very light cranberry #605 Lazy Daisy	
⊘ Dark cornflower blue #798 Lazy Daisy	
⊘ Blue #799 Lazy Daisy	

Color numbers given are for Coats & Clark Red Heart Classic yarn Art. E267 and DMC #3 pearl cotton.

Vanity Tray Short Side
69 holes x 12 holes
Cut 2

Vanity Tray Long Side
89 holes x 12 holes
Cut 2

Continue pattern

Cut out

Jewelry Box Lid Top
33 holes x 37 holes
Cut 1

Continue pattern around tray

Continue pattern

Vanity Tray Bottom
89 holes x 69 holes
Cut 1

VICTORIAN LAMP SHADE

Give your bedroom a touch of Victoriana with this elegant lamp shade. Pastel accents stitched on a white background, finished off with fringe, will suit any decor.

Experience Level: Intermediate

Materials
- 3 sheets 7-count stiff plastic canvas
- Plastic canvas yarn as listed in color key
- 1⅔ yards 4"-long white fringe
- Fabric glue
- 5"-diameter clamp-on-the-bulb lamp shade ring
- Purchased lamp base

Instructions

1. Cut plastic canvas according to graphs.

2. Stitch pieces following graphs. Using white through step 5, Overcast top edges of lamp shade tops and bottom edges of lamp shade bottoms. Overcast side edges of lamp shade bottoms except straight edges between blue dots.

3. Whipstitch bottom edge of one top piece to top edge of one bottom piece. Repeat with remaining top and bottom pieces. With wrong sides together, Whipstitch two shade pieces together between blue dots. Open up pieces and Whipstitch together at points indicated with red dots. Whipstitch top sides together.

4. Repeat three more times until there are four pairs, then Whipstitch pairs together, forming shade.

5. At every two holes, Whipstitch lamp shade ring to inside seam where top and bottom pieces meet.

6. Glue fringe to inside bottom scalloped edge.

—Designed by Carole Rodgers

COLOR KEY	
Plastic Canvas Yarn	**Yards**
■ Sail blue #35	25
▨ Baby blue #36	50
☐ White #41	92
Color numbers given are for Uniek Needloft plastic canvas yarn.	

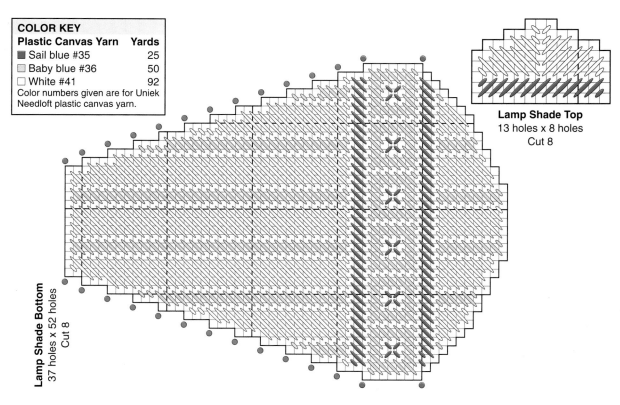

Lamp Shade Top
13 holes x 8 holes
Cut 8

Lamp Shade Bottom
37 holes x 52 holes
Cut 8

Forget-Me-Not Bouquet

*Keeping your jewelry organized and tidy has never been so easy or
so decorative as with this colorful earring caddy and jewelry box.*

Experience Level: Advanced

Materials

- 2 sheets 7-count stiff plastic canvas
- 1 sheet 7-count clear plastic canvas
- Worsted weight yarn as listed in color key
- Ribbon floss as listed in color key
- 9" x 12" sheet self-adhesive white felt
- 1¾" x 1¾" gold filigree heart
- 2 (11") lengths ⅛"-diameter wooden dowel

Cutting & Stitching

1. Cut tray sides and trinket box front from regular plastic canvas; cut ladders, ladder support tops, tray base, trinket box lid and trinket box bottom from stiff plastic canvas according to graphs (pages 136–138).

2. From regular plastic canvas, cut two 5-hole by 6-hole pieces for tray splices. From stiff plastic canvas, cut one 48-hole x 14-hole piece for box back, four 10-hole x 3-hole pieces for ladder support sides and four 6-hole x 3-hole pieces for ladder support ends.

3. Cut two pieces of felt slightly smaller than tray sides. Cut one piece felt slightly smaller than box lid.

4. Stitch pieces following graphs. Do not stitch ladder rungs or areas indicated with yellow lines on ladder and tray base graphs at this time. To connect the two tray side pieces to form a circle, center tray splices behind short edges of two tray side pieces before stitching, then Continental Stitch with white through both thicknesses.

5. With white, Continental Stitch box back and ladder support sides and ends.

6. Over completed Continental Stitches, Backstitch with 2 plies china rose and 4 plies lark lagoon. Use 4 plies periwinkle and light periwinkle for forget-me-knot French Knots. Work ribbon floss embroidery, wrapping floss around needle once for wild rose French

Knots and twice for forget-me-not French Knots.

Earring Caddy Assembly

1. Place wrong sides of ladder pieces together with wooden dowel between the two vertical posts. Using white through step 4, Whipstitch inner and outer edges of ladder pieces together, Continental Stitching areas indicated with yellow lines. Following graph, stitch ladder rungs through both thicknesses.

2. Overcast inside edges of support tops. Whipstitch side edges of two support ends to side edges of two support sides, forming a box. Whipstitch box to one support top. Repeat with remaining support pieces. Overcast bottom edges of support box.

3. Insert bottom of posts in openings of support top, stopping at bottom of first forget-me-not. Whipstitch bottom of posts to tray base where indicated with yellow lines. Tack support sides and ends to tray base at several points.

4. Overcast top edge of tray side. Attach felt to tray side, placing ends of felt at splices. Whipstitch side to base, centering spliced areas on short ends of tray base.

Trinket Box Assembly

1. Using white through step 3, Overcast top edge of box front. Whipstitch side edges of box front and back together. With right side of box bottom on the inside, Whipstitch front and back to box bottom.

2. Making sure wrong side of lid is to the inside, center straight edge of box lid on top edge of box back; Whipstitch together, making sure to not pull stitches too tightly.

3. Overcast remaining edges of box lid, attaching filigree heart to lid where indicated on graph while Overcasting. Attach felt to wrong side of lid.

— Designed by Darla Fanton

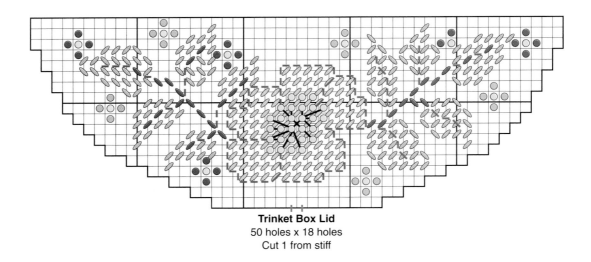

Trinket Box Lid
50 holes x 18 holes
Cut 1 from stiff

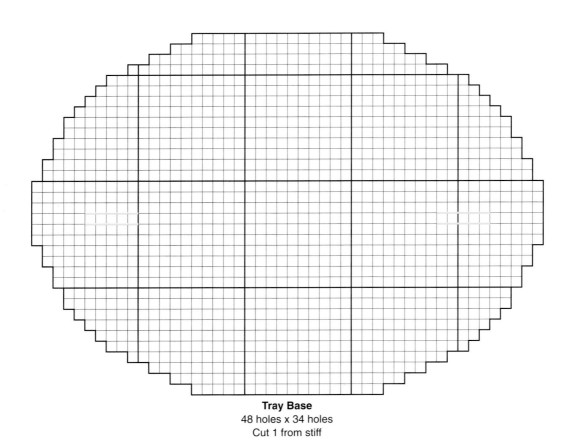

Tray Base
48 holes x 34 holes
Cut 1 from stiff

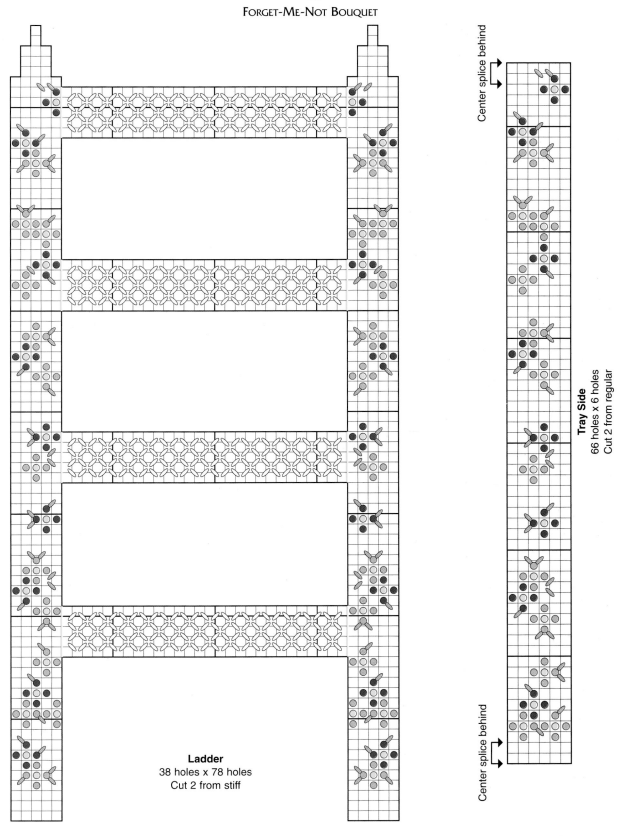

Ladder
38 holes x 78 holes
Cut 2 from stiff

Tray Side
66 holes x 6 holes
Cut 2 from regular

Center splice behind

Center splice behind

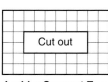

Ladder Support Top
10 holes x 6 holes
Cut 2 from stiff

Cut out

Trinket Box Front
66 holes x 14 holes
Cut 1 from regular

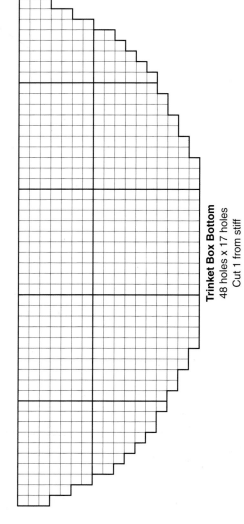

Trinket Box Bottom
48 holes x 17 holes
Cut 1 from stiff

COLOR KEY

Worsted Weight Yarn	Yards
▦ Medium lagoon #8821	8
■ Dark lagoon #8822	2
▢ Rose #8921	2
▨ Arbutus #8922	1
□ White #8942	103

Uncoded areas are white #8942
Continental Stitches

/ Dark lagoon #8822 Backstitch	
/ China rose #8923 Backstitch	1
● Light periwinkle #8803 French Knot	6
● Periwinkle #8804 French Knot	6

Ribbon Floss

/ Yellow #142F13 Backstitch	12
○ Yellow #142F13 French Knot	
‖ Attach filigree heart	

Color numbers given are for Spinrite Bernat Berella "4" worsted weight yarn and Rhode Island Textile RibbonFloss.

CLIMBING FLOWERS

Delicate embroidered flowers climbing up the sides of this
wastepaper basket make this lovely piece a perfect bedroom accent.

Experience Level: Intermediate

Materials
- 2 sheets 7-count stiff plastic canvas
- Worsted weight yarn as listed in color key
- #3 pearl cotton as listed in color key
- 1½ yards ⅞"-wide single-faced peach satin ribbon
- Hot-glue gun

Instructions

1. Cut sides and bottom from plastic canvas according to graphs (below and page 140).

2. Stitch pieces with yarn following graphs. Work embroidery over completed Alternating Continental Stitches following embroidery chart.

3. Overcast top edges of basket sides with light mint and inside edges of basket sides with mint. With light mint, Whipstitch sides together then Whipstitch sides to bottom.

4. Using photo as a guide and making sure satin side is toward the front, weave ribbon through cutouts and over corners. Begin by threading ribbon from front to back through one center cutout of one side, out through side cutout and over corner, in through next side cutout, out through first center cutout and in through second cutout. Continue weaving pattern until ribbon has been woven through entire basket.

5. Make ends of ribbon even and tie in a bow. Secure knot with hot glue.

—Designed by Celia Lange Designs

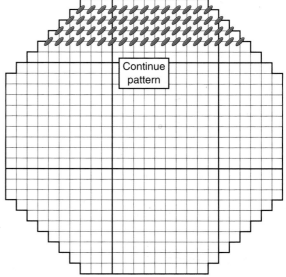

Wastepaper Basket Bottom
26 holes x 26 holes
Cut 1

COLOR KEY	
Worsted Weight Yarn	**Yards**
☐ White #311	23
▨ Light mint #364	35
■ Mint #366	52
#3 Pearl Cotton	
○ Pale yellow #745 French Knot	10
◔ Light salmon #761 French Knot	10
⟁ Salmon #760 Lazy Daisy	18
╱ Dark blue green #991 Backstitch	17
Color numbers given are for Coats & Clark Red Heart Super Saver yarn Art. E301 and DMC #3 pearl cotton.	

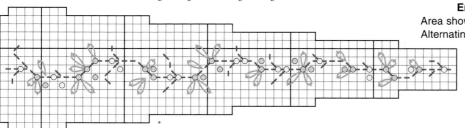

Embroidery Chart
Area shown is light mint and white
Alternating Continental Stitch area

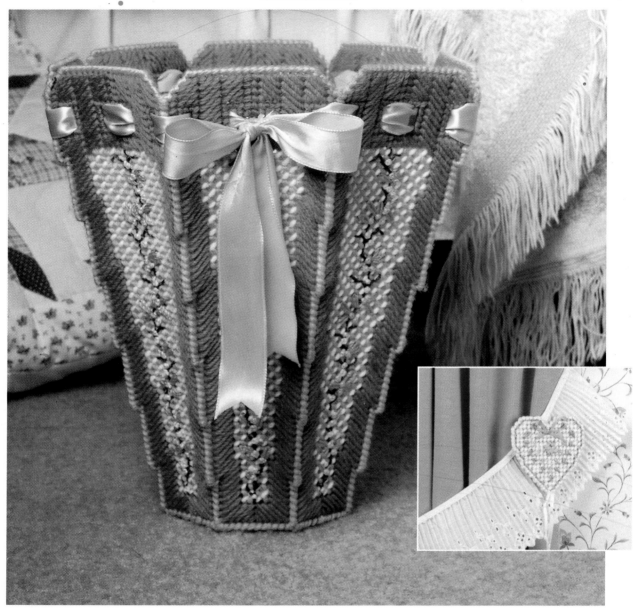

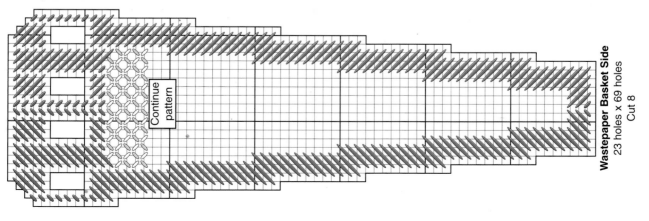

Continue pattern

Wastepaper Basket Side
23 holes x 69 holes
Cut 8

HEART TIEBACK

*With just a few quick and easy stitches, you can have a pretty curtain tieback.
It looks especially attractive on Battenburg or lace ruffled curtains.*

Experience Level: Intermediate

Materials

- 4" square 7-count plastic canvas
- 6-strand embroidery floss as listed in color key
- 4mm silk embroidery ribbon as listed in color key
- 7mm silk embroidery ribbon as listed in color key
- #18 or #20 tapestry needle
- 15" ⅛"-wide ecru satin ribbon
- 4" square ecru felt
- 2 (6mm) ecru faceted beads
- Curtain tieback or desired length 3"-wide eyelet trim or lace
- White craft glue

Instructions

1. Cut heart from plastic canvas according to graph. Using heart as a template, cut felt slightly smaller than plastic canvas heart.

2. Continental Stitch and Overcast heart with 18 strands ecru floss following graph.

3. Work French Knots and Backstitches when Continental Stitching and Overcasting are completed. Work pink and blue French Knots, wrapping ribbon around needle four times; work lavender French Knots, wrapping ribbon around needle two times. Work each blue and lavender French Knot on right side of heart in opposite direction of ecru stitch below it; work each blue and lavender French Knot on left side of heart in same direction as ecru stitch below it.

4. For bow, cut a 6" length of green embroidery ribbon. Thread ends from back to front through holes indicated on graph. Tie ribbon in a bow, trimming ends as desired. Glue bow to heart to secure.

5. Thread ⅛"-wide ecru satin ribbon from back to front through two bottom holes on heart. Make

ends equal in length. Glue ribbon to back of heart to secure.

6. Tie a loose knot approximately every inch along both lengths of ecru ribbon until there are four knots on each length. Slide ecru bead on end of each length and tie a knot in each end; apply a dot of glue to both knots. Slide beads down over knots so knots are concealed inside beads.

7. Apply a small amount of glue to outer edge of felt backing and glue firmly in place on back of heart. Using photo as a guide, tack heart to tieback at center top of heart with 6 strands ecru floss.

—Designed by Kathleen Marie O'Donnell

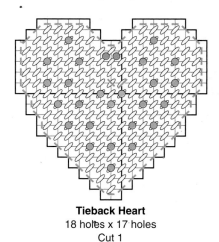

Tieback Heart
18 holes x 17 holes
Cut 1

COLOR KEY	
6-Strand Embroidery Floss	**Skeins**
☐ Ecru	2
7mm Silk Embroidery Ribbon	**Yards**
⬤ Pink French Knot	⅔
4mm Silk Embroidery Ribbon	
⬤ Blue French Knot	1
⬤ Lavender French Knot	⅔
╱ Light green Backstitch	1
⬤ Attach bow	

STRIPED BED CADDY

Slide this clever caddy between your mattress and bedspring for easy access to a TV remote, magazines, your eyeglasses or other small items.

Experience Level: Advanced beginner

Materials
- 3 sheets 7-count soft plastic canvas
- Worsted weight yarn as listed in color key
- #16 tapestry needle
- 3½ yards ⅛"-wide pale blue satin ribbon

Instructions

1. Cut plastic canvas according to graphs (below and page 144). Cut one 83-hole x 70-hole piece for caddy flap, one 83-hole x 2-hole piece for bottom gusset and two 2-hole by 52-hole pieces for side gussets.

2. Stitch top portion of caddy back following graph. Bottom portion below yellow line will remain unstitched. With light damson, Continental Stitch all three gussets. Caddy flap will remain unstitched.

3. Stitch caddy front following graph, leaving center strip of winter white Slanting Gobelin Stitches unworked for now. Stitch pale navy flower centers first in one direction, then stitch over these stitches in the opposite direction.

4. Cut a 1-yard length of ribbon and thread one end through needle; knot remaining end. Keeping ribbon flat, thread ribbon under the three vertical rows of winter white Cross Stitches and Straight Stitches on left side of caddy front. Repeat for right side of caddy front.

5. Repeat process with remaining ribbon, threading ribbon under two rows of winter white Cross Stitches and Straight Stitches on top portion of caddy back.

6. Using pale damson throughout, Whipstitch bottom gusset to bottom edges of caddy front and back. Whipstitch side gussets to side edges of caddy front and back, Overcasting remaining side edges of caddy back while Whipstitching. Whipstitch side gussets to bottom gusset.

7. Using winter white throughout, Overcast top edges of side gussets and caddy front. Following caddy front graph, stitch center portion of caddy front to caddy back with Slanting Gobelin Stitches, forming two pockets. Whipstitch top edge of caddy back to one long side of caddy flap.

8. Insert flap between bedspring and mattress, allowing stitched section to hang along side of bed.

—Designed by Joan Green

Top

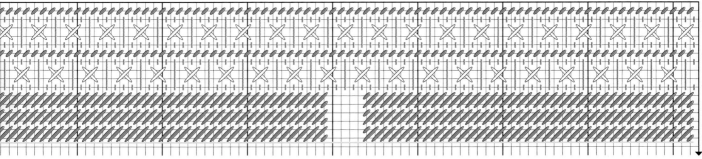

Bed Caddy Back
83 holes x 63 holes
Cut 1

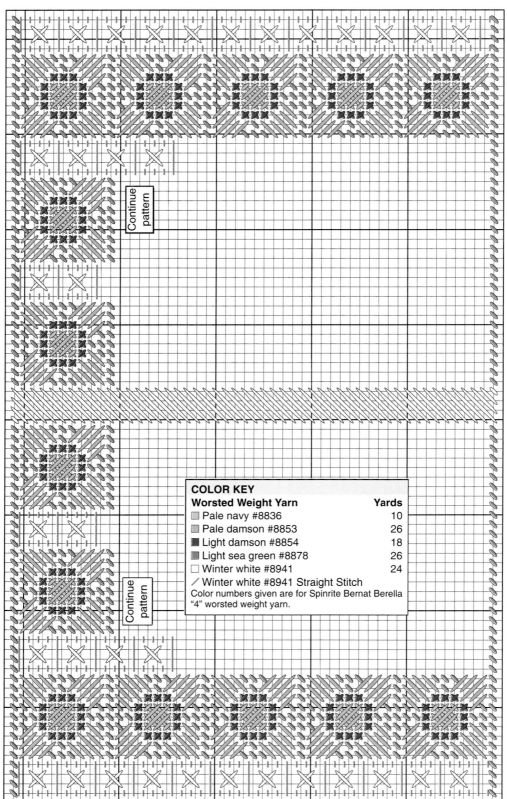

Continue pattern

Continue pattern

Bed Caddy Front
83 holes x 52 holes
Cut 1

COLOR KEY	
Worsted Weight Yarn	**Yards**
▨ Pale navy #8836	10
▨ Pale damson #8853	26
■ Light damson #8854	18
▨ Light sea green #8878	26
☐ Winter white #8941	24
╱ Winter white #8941 Straight Stitch	

Color numbers given are for Spinrite Bernat Berella "4" worsted weight yarn.

TULIP TREASURES

Stitched in black with fuchsia and green sparkling accents, this hand mirror and jewelry box set is simply gorgeous!

Experience Level: Intermediate

Project Note

When working with metallic ribbon, keep ribbon smooth and flat. To prevent twisting and tangling, guide ribbon between thumb and forefinger of free hand. Drop needle occasionally to let ribbon unwind.

JEWELRY BOX

Materials

- 1 sheet 10-count plastic canvas
- #3 pearl cotton as listed in color key
- ⅛"-wide metallic ribbon as listed in color key
- #22 tapestry needle
- 17mm coordinating square acrylic stone (sample used mint)
- Adhesive-backed black felt
- Craft glue

Instructions

1. Cut plastic canvas according to graphs (page 149). Cut four 29-hole x 5-hole pieces for lid sides and one 32-hole x 32-hole piece for box bottom.

2. Following project note and graphs, stitch plastic canvas following graphs. One lid top, lid sides and box bottom will remain unstitched.

3. Using black pearl cotton through step 4, Whipstitch lid sides together. Whipstitch lid sides to unstitched lid top where indicated on graph. Place stitched lid top on unstitched lid top and Whipstitch together.

4. Overcast top edges of box sides. Whipstitch box sides together, then Whipstitch sides to box bottom.

5. Cut one 3⅛" square from black felt and attach to inside box bottom. Cut one 2¹³⁄₁₆" square from black felt and attach to inside lid. Glue acrylic stone to center of tulip design on lid top.

HAND MIRROR

Materials

- 1 sheet 10-count plastic canvas
- #3 pearl cotton as listed in color key
- ⅛"-wide metallic ribbon as listed in color key
- #22 tapestry needle
- 17mm coordinating square acrylic stone (sample used mint)
- 5" round mirror
- 9" 1"-wide wooden paint-stirring stick
- Hot-glue gun

Instructions

1. Cut plastic canvas according to graphs (pages 147 and 148). Cut one 1-hole by 15-hole strip for mirror top and two 134-hole x 1-hole strips for mirror sides.

2. Following project note and graphs, stitch plastic canvas following graphs. With green ribbon, Overcast inside edges of mirror front. Mirror sides and mirror top will remain unstitched.

3. Using black pearl cotton through step 4 and starting at center bottom of handle, Whipstitch one mirror side to mirror back, ending at red dot on mirror back graph; trim excess holes from side as necessary. Repeat with remaining mirror side. Whipstitch mirror top to top edge of mirror back.

4. Whipstitch handle only of front piece to sides. Insert stick into handle, then glue mirror to stick, making sure mirror is centered in opening. Whipstitch remaining edges of mirror front to side and top pieces.

5. Glue acrylic stone to center of tulip design on mirror back.

—Designed by Kathy Wirth

COLOR KEY

#3 Pearl Cotton	Yards
■ Black #403	59
⅛" **Ribbon**	
■ Green #008	12
■ Fuchsia #024	10
□ Pearl #032	12

╱ Whipstitch to lid sides

Color numbers given are for Anchor #3 pearl cotton by Coats & Clark and Kreinik ⅛" Ribbon.

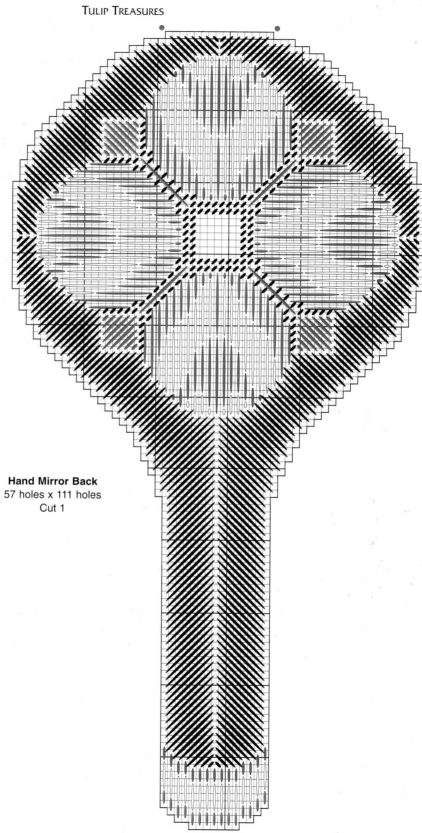

Hand Mirror Back
57 holes x 111 holes
Cut 1

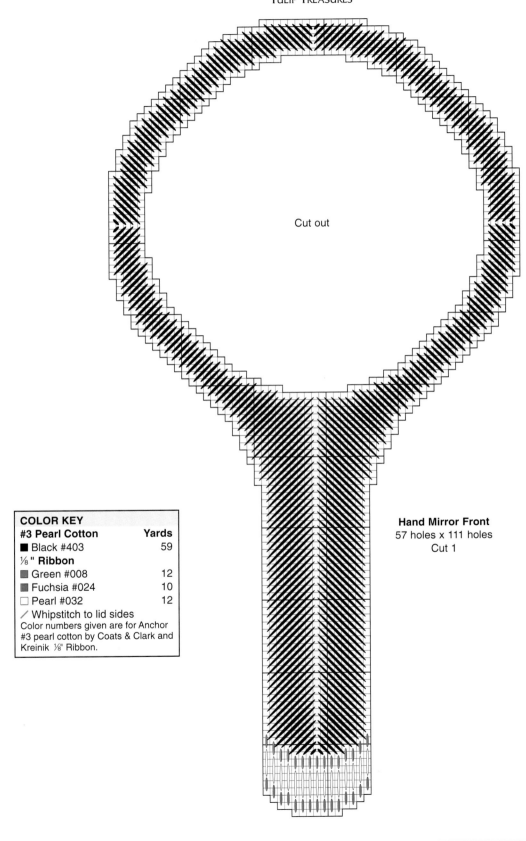

Cut out

COLOR KEY

#3 Pearl Cotton	Yards
■ Black #403	59
⅛" **Ribbon**	
▨ Green #008	12
▨ Fuchsia #024	10
☐ Pearl #032	12

╱ Whipstitch to lid sides
Color numbers given are for Anchor
#3 pearl cotton by Coats & Clark and
Kreinik ⅛" Ribbon.

Hand Mirror Front
57 holes x 111 holes
Cut 1

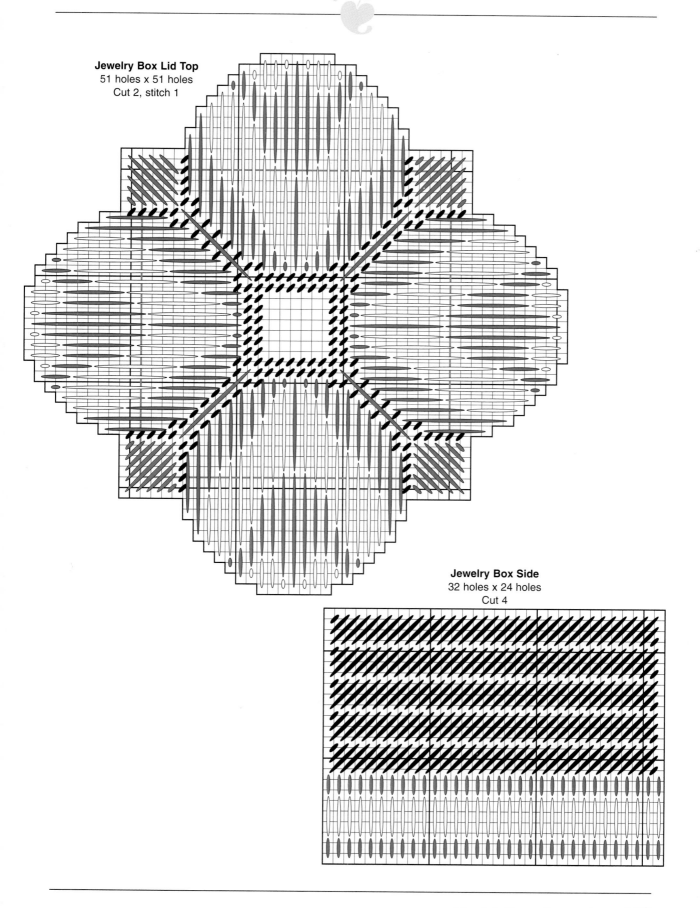

Jewelry Box Lid Top
51 holes x 51 holes
Cut 2, stitch 1

Jewelry Box Side
32 holes x 24 holes
Cut 4

VICTORIAN BOUQUET

A bountiful bouquet of flowers, stitched on 10-count
plastic canvas with pearl cotton, adorns a large box
and coordinating switch-plate cover.

Experience Level: Intermediate

BOUTIQUE BOX

Materials
- 1½ sheets 10-count plastic canvas
- 6-strand embroidery floss as listed in color key
- #18 or #20 tapestry needle
- 2 (9" x 12") pieces ivory felt
- White glue

Instructions

1. Cut pieces from plastic canvas according to graphs (below and pages 152 and 153). Cut one 83-hole x 30-hole piece for box bottom.

2. Using plastic canvas pieces as templates, cut two pieces felt slightly smaller than box bottom and one piece felt each slightly smaller than box sides, lid top and lid sides. For lid sides, cut pieces only ½" wide, omitting scallops.

3. Stitch pieces with 12 strands floss following graphs. Box bottom will remain unstitched.

4. Using ecru throughout, Overcast bottom edges of lid sides and top edges of box sides. Whipstitch lid sides together, then Whipstitch lid sides to lid top. Whipstitch box sides together, then Whipstitch box sides to box bottom.

5. Glue felt lining in lid and box, gluing one piece felt to both top and bottom of box bottom.

SWITCH-PLATE COVER

Materials
- ¼ sheet 10-count plastic canvas
- 6-strand embroidery floss as listed in color key
- #18 or #20 tapestry needle
- 3⅞" x 5¾" acrylic switch-plate cover
- 4" x 6" piece fusible interfacing (optional)

Instructions

1. Cut plastic canvas according to graph (page 154). ***Note:*** *If necessary, change holes on plastic canvas to match holes on acrylic cover.*

2. If lining is desired, use plastic canvas as a pattern to cut out iron-on lining, cutting holes for switch and screws.

3. With 12 strands floss, Continental Stitch piece following graph. Backstitch with 6 strands floss. With 12 strands ecru, Overcast corners only.

4. If desired, iron interfacing to backside of finished piece, following manufacturer's directions.

5. Place stitched piece in acrylic cover.

—Designed by Kathleen Marie O'Donnell

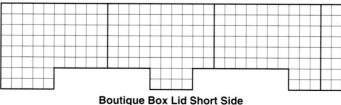

Boutique Box Lid Short Side
32 holes x 8 holes
Cut 2

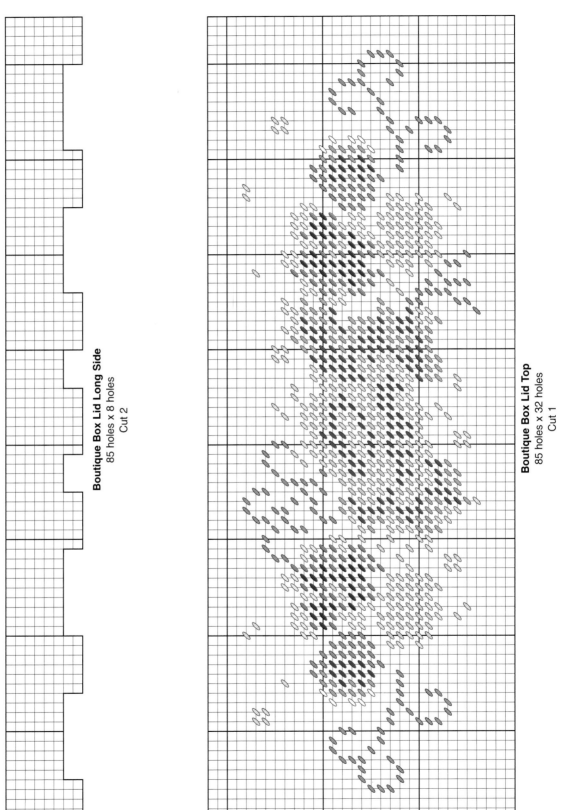

Boutique Box Lid Long Side
85 holes x 8 holes
Cut 2

Boutique Box Lid Top
85 holes x 32 holes
Cut 1

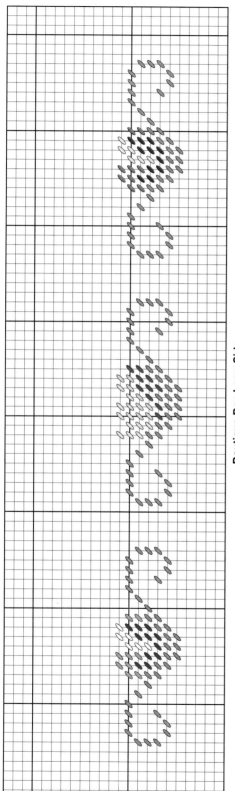

Boutique Box Long Side
83 holes x 23 holes
Cut 2

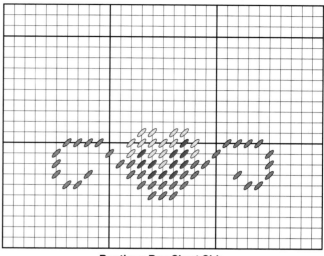

Boutique Box Short Side
30 holes x 23 holes
Cut 2

COLOR KEY	
BOUTIQUE BOX	
6-Strand Embroidery Floss	**Skeins**
■ Medium lavender #208	1
▨ Medium light lavender #209	1
□ Light lavender #211	1
■ Dark pistachio green #367	1
▨ Light pistachio green #368	1
□ Very light pistachio green #369	1
▨ Blue green #502	2
□ Wheat straw #676	1
■ Medium royal blue #797	1
▨ Blue #799	1
□ Pale delft #800	1
■ Very dark dusty rose #3350	1
▨ Medium mauve #3688	2
□ Light mauve #3689	1
Uncoded areas are ecru	
Continental Stitches	22
Color numbers given are for DMC 6-strand embroidery floss.	

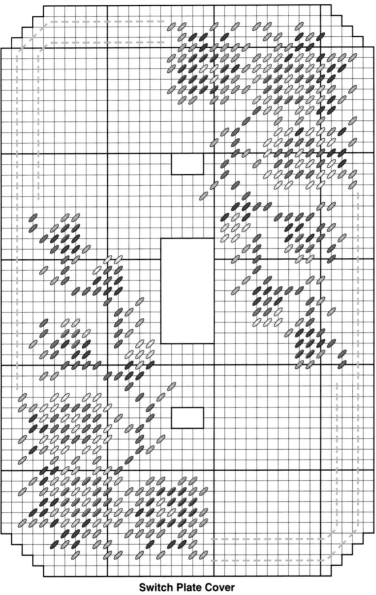

Switch Plate Cover
35 holes x 54 holes
Cut 1

COLOR KEY	
SWITCH-PLATE COVER	
6-Strand Embroidery Floss	**Skeins**
■ Dark pistachio green #367	1
▨ Light pistachio green #368	1
■ Medium mustard #370	1
▨ Medium violet #552	1
■ Dark lavender #554	1
☐ Wheat straw #676	1
☐ Very light topaz #727	1
■ Medium blue #826	1
☐ Very light blue #827	1
▨ Light melon #3326	1
■ Medium dark dusty rose #3731	1
Uncoded areas are ecru	
Continental Stitches	3
╱ Light pistachio green #368	
Backstitch	
Color numbers given are for DMC 6-strand embroidery floss.	

STITCH GUIDE

Use the following diagrams to expand your plastic canvas stitching. For each diagram, bring needle up through canvas at the red number one and go back down through the canvas at the red number two. The second stitch is numbered in green. Always bring needle up through the canvas at odd numbers and take it back down through the canvas at the even numbers.

BACKGROUND STITCHES

The following stitches are used for filling in large areas of canvas. The Continental Stitch is the most commonly used stitch. Other stitches, such as the Condensed Mosaic and Scotch Stitch, fill in large areas of canvas more quickly than the Continental Stitch because their stitches cover a larger area of canvas.

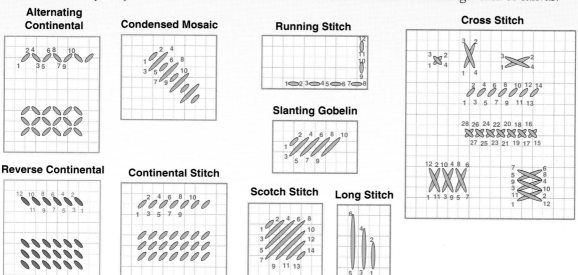

EMBROIDERY STITCHES

Embroidery stitches are worked on top of a stitched area to add detail and beauty to your project. Embroidery stitches are usually worked with one strand of yarn, several strands of pearl cotton or several strands of embroidery floss.

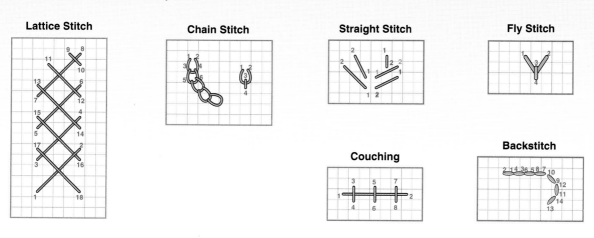

EMBROIDERY STITCHES

French Knot

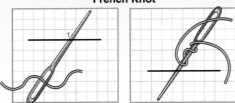

Bring needle up through piece. Wrap yarn around needle 2 or 3 times, depending on desired size of knot; take needle back through piece through same hole.

Lazy Daisy

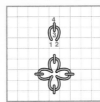

Bring yarn needle up through canvas, then back down in same hole, leaving a small loop.

Then, bring needle up inside loop; take needle back down through piece on other side of loop.

SPECIALTY STITCHES

The following stitches can be worked either on top of a previously stitched area or directly onto the canvas. Like the embroidery stitches, these too add wonderful detail and give your stitching additional interest and texture.

Diamond Eyelet

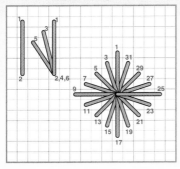

For each stitch, bring needle up at odd numbers around outside and take needle down through canvas at center hole.

Smyrna Cross

Satin Stitch

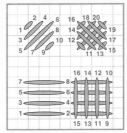

This stitch gives a "padded" look to your work.

FINISHING STITCHES

Both of these stitches are used to finish the outer edges of the canvas. Overcasting is done to finish one edge at a time. Whipstitch is used to stitch two pieces of canvas together. For both Overcasting and Whipstitching, work one stitch in each hole along straight edges and inside corners, and two or three stitches in outside corners.

Overcast/Whipstitch

Loop Stitch or Turkey Loop Stitch

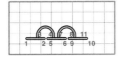

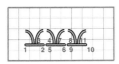

The top diagram shows this stitch left intact. This is an effective stitch for giving a project dimensional hair. The bottom diagram demonstrates the cut loop stitch. Because each stitch is anchored, cutting it will not cause the stitches to come out. A group of cut loop stitches gives a fluffy, soft look and feel to your project.

ACKNOWLEDGMENTS

Our gratitude is extended to all who opened up their homes and for the photography of this book. The beautiful locations added warmth and charm to the photographs. We'd also like to thank the following manufacturers who have generously provided our designers with materials and supplies. We appreciate their contribution to the production of this book.

Coats & Clark
Craft & Yarn Division
30 Patewood Dr.
Greenville, SC 29615
(803) 234–0331

- Anchor #3 pearl cotton—Quilt Coasters, Tulip Treasures
- J. & P. Coats plastic canvas yarn Article E.46—Lodge-Look Desk Set
- Red Heart® Classic™ yarn Art. E267—Backgammon Set, Classic Vanity Set, Magazine Holder, Revolving Organizer, Arts Magnet Collection
- Red Heart® Super Saver yarn Art. E301—Climbing Flowers

Darice mail order:
Bolek's Craft Supplys Inc.
P.O. Box 465
330 N. Tuscarawas Ave.
Dover, OH 44622-0465
(216) 364–8878

- 3" plastic canvas radial circle—Classic Vanity Set
- 6" plastic canvas radial circle—Nut Basket Set
- Music bank—Teddy Bear Musical Bank
- Nylon Plus plastic canvas yarn—Balloon Bear Set
- Plastic canvas—Country Kitchen, Maple Leaf Table Set, Nut Basket Set, Ivy House Sign, Cheerful Plant Pokes, Coupon Keepers, Revolving Organizer, I Love Crafts, Lodge-Look Desk Set, Nursery Rhyme Time, Balloon Bear Set, Roses, Roses, Tissue Keeper, Forget-Me-Not Bouquet
- Super Soft™ plastic canvas—Crayon Photo Frame, Striped Bed Caddy
- Ultra Stiff™ plastic canvas—Herb Planter, Sugar 'n' Spice, Backgammon Set, Magazine Holder, Revolving Organizer, Octagonal Quilt Box, Computer Disk Caddy, Teddy Bear Musical Bank, Crayon Photo Frame, Roses, Roses, Classic Vanity Set, Forget-Me-Not Bouquet, Climbing Flowers

The DMC Corp.
10 Port Kearny
South Kearny, NJ 07032
(201) 589–0606

- 6-strand embroidery floss—Floral Mugs, Fruit Coaster Set, Coupon Keepers, Nursery Rhyme Time (mobile), Balloon Bear Set, Tropical Treasures, Graceful Swan, Heart Tieback, Under the Sea, Victorian Bouquet
- #3 pearl cotton—Herb Planter, Sugar 'n' Spice, Nut Basket Set, Do Not Disturb, Classic Vanity Set, Climbing Flowers
- #5 pearl cotton—Sunflower Welcome, Teddy Bear Musical Bank

Fibre-Craft Materials Corp.
6310 W. Touhy Ave.
Niles, IL 60714
(708) 647–1140

- Doll stand—Cooking Angel

Kreinik Mfg. Co. Inc.
3106 Timanus Ln.
Baltimore, MD 21244
(410) 281–0040

- ⅛" Ribbon—Tulip Treasures
- 8-ply Ombre—Tropical Treasures

Kunin Felt Co./Foss Mfg. Co. Inc.
380 Lafayette Rd.
P.O. Box 5000
Hampton, NH 03842
(800) 292–7900

- Presto Felt™—Forget-Me-Not Bouquet

Lion Brand Yarn Co.
34 W. 15th St.
New York, NY 10011
(212) 243–8995

- Chenille yarn—Teddy Bear Musical Bank

Mill Hill Products
Gay Bowles Sales, Inc.
P.O. Box 1060
Janesville, WI 53547
(608) 754–9466

- Ceramic button—Cooking Angel, Octagonal Quilt Box

ACKNOWLEDGMENTS

MPR Associates, Inc.
P.O. Box 7343
High Point, NC 27264
(800) 334–1047

- Satin Raffia Ribbon—Cheerful Plant Pokes

Provo Craft
285 E 900 S
Provo, UT 84606
(800) 937–7686

- Create O'Clock clock movement—Classic Vanity Set

Rainbow Gallery mail order:
Designs by Joan Green
6345 Fairfield Rd.
Oxford, OH 45056
(513) 523–2690

- Plastic Canvas 7 Metallic Yarn—Magazine Holder, Arts Magnet Collection (Quill, Stage Bill), Sparkling Seashells
- Plastic Canvas 10 Metallic Yarn—Magazine Holder, Rosebuds & Lace

Rhode Island Textile Co.
P.O. Box 999
Pawtucket, RI 02862
(401) 722–3700

- RibbonFloss™—Forget-Me-Not Bouquet

Shafaii Co.
1000 Broadway
Houston, TX 77012
(713) 923–5300

- Filigree heart—Forget-Me-Not Bouquet

Spinrite, Inc.
Box 40
Listowel, Ont., N4W 3H3

- Plastic canvas yarn—Herb Planter, Sugar 'n' Spice, Garden-Fresh Caddies, Nut Basket Set, Summertime Swings
- Bernat® Berella "4"® worsted weight yarn—Country Kitchen, Cooking Angel, Bless Our Home, Ivy House Sign, Welcome Wreath, Computer Disk Caddy, I Love Crafts, Octagonal Quilt Box, Summertime Swings, Sparkling Seashells, Forget-Me-Not Bouquet, Rosebuds & Lace, Striped Bed Caddy

Toner Plastics, Inc.
668 Dickinson St.
Springfield, MA 01108
(413) 733–8629

- Glow In Dark CraftLace™—Nursery Rhyme Time

Uniek Inc.
P.O. Box 457
805 Uniek Dr.
Waunakee, WI 53597
(608) 849–9999

- Stiff plastic canvas—Chicken Little, Victorian Lamp Shade
- Needloft® plastic canvas yarn—Chicken Little, Message Center, Cheerful Plant Pokes, Coupon Keepers, Nursery Rhyme Time, Teddy Bear Musical Bank, Crayon Photo Frame, Roses, Roses, Tissue Keeper, Victorian Lamp Shade

Westrim Crafts
9667 Canoga Ave.
P.O. Box 3879
Chatsworth, CA 91313
(818) 998–8550

- Fun Foam—Nut Basket Set, Classic Vanity Set

Wm. E. Wright
85 South St.
Bountiful, UT 84010
(801) 298–0504

- Roses Per Yard—Rosebuds & Lace

SPECIAL THANKS

*The publishers and editorial staff of
Heart & Home Expressions would like to give recognition to
each of the designers whose marvelous designs have filled the
pages of this plastic canvas craft book.*

Angie Arickx
Coupon Keepers, Roses, Roses, Tissue Keeper

Martha Bleidner & Celia Lange of Celia Lange Designs
Herb Planter, Sugar 'n' Spice, Backgammon Set, Magazine
Holder, Nut Basket Set, Revolving Organizer,
Classic Vanity Set, Climbing Flowers

Darla Fanton
Forget-Me-Not Bouquet

Conn Baker Gibney
Arts Magnet Collection

Joan Green
Cooking Angel, Country Kitchen, Bless Our Home, Ivy House
Sign, Welcome Wreath, Computer Disk Caddy, I Love Crafts,
Octagonal Quilt Box, Summertime Swings, Rosebuds & Lace,
Sparkling Seashells, Striped Bed Caddy

Kathleen Kennebeck
Nursery Rhyme Time

Carol Krob
Garden-Fresh Caddies

Cherie Marie Leck
Teddy Bear Musical Bank

Nancy Marshall
Maple Leaf Table Set, Lodge-Look Desk Set, Balloon Bear Set

Adele Mogavero
Cheerful Plant Pokes

Kathleen Marie O'Donnell
Floral Mugs, Fruit Coaster Set, Tropical Treasures,
Graceful Swan, Do Not Disturb, Under the Sea,
Heart Tieback, Victorian Bouquet

Carole Rodgers
Chicken Little, Victorian Lamp Shade

Kathy Wirth
Message Center, Quilt Coasters, Sunflower Welcome,
Crayon Photo Frame, Tulip Treasures

INDEX